Is Just War Possible?

T0045602

Political Theory Today

Janna Thompson, *Should Current Generations Make Reparations for Slavery?*

Christopher Bertram, *Do States Have the Right to Exclude Immigrants?*

Diana Coole, *Should We Control World Population?*

Christopher Finlay, *Is Just War Possible?*

Christopher Finlay

———

Is Just War Possible?

polity

Copyright © Christopher Finlay 2019

L E V E R H U L M E
T R U S T _____

The right of Christopher Finlay to be identified as Author of this Work has been
asserted in accordance with the UK Copyright, Designs and Patents Act 1988.

First published in 2019 by Polity Press

Polity Press
65 Bridge Street
Cambridge CB2 1UR, UK

Polity Press
101 Station Landing
Suite 300
Medford, MA 02155, USA

ISBN-13: 978-1-5095-2649-9
ISBN-13: 978-1-5095-2650-5 (pb)

A catalogue record for this book is available from the British Library.

Library of Congress Cataloging-in-Publication Data
Names: Finlay, Christopher (Christopher J.), author.
Title: Is just war possible? / Christopher Finlay.
Description: Cambridge, UK ; Medford, MA, USA : Polity Press, 2018. | Series:
    Political theory today | Includes bibliographical references and index.
Identifiers: LCCN 2018012984 (print) | LCCN 2018028626 (ebook) | ISBN
    9781509526536 (Epub) | ISBN 9781509526499 (hardback) | ISBN 9781509526505
    (pbk.)
Subjects: LCSH: Just war doctrine.
Classification: LCC U22 (ebook) | LCC U22 .F559 2018 (print) | DDC
    172/.42--dc23
LC record available at https://lccn.loc.gov/2018012984

Typeset in 11 on 15 Sabon by Servis Filmsetting Ltd, Stockport, Cheshire
Printed and bound in the United Kingdom by Clays Ltd, Elcograph S.p.A

For further information on Polity, visit our website:
politybooks.com

For my parents

Contents

Preface   viii
Acknowledgements   xv

1 Ideas and Ideals of the Just War   1
2 The Just War Creed   19
3 'Just Cause' and the Possibility of *Jus ad
   Bellum*   33
4 Fighting Just Wars: Balancing Ends and
   Means   72
5 Conclusion: Just Wars, Ideal and Non-
   Ideal   97

Notes   105
References   109

Preface

When thousands of people gathered in cities across Britain in November 2015 to protest against proposals to bomb Daesh in Syria, many expressed exasperation at the government's failure to learn from the wars in Afghanistan and Iraq. Neither bombers and missiles nor soldiers on the ground had succeeded in bringing peace and justice to those states when they were deployed soon after 9/11. Nor did they succeed later when used to support anti-Gaddafi rebels in Libya in 2011. The protesters of 2015 therefore believed that those millions of their predecessors who had turned out in 2002 and 2003 to oppose Tony Blair and George W. Bush had been proven right.

But what exactly was the message that government ministers should have been listening to? And what was the lesson they should have learnt? I myself was part of those earlier protests. By 2002, I was increasingly worried by what seemed to me to be a dangerously misguided foreign policy. The impending Iraq intervention didn't seem justified by a well-founded fear of attack. More especially, I thought that invading another country with a view to changing its regime from an authoritarian one to a constitutional democracy was wrongheaded. Even though the intended outcome was a worthy one, as I was prepared to accept, it seemed to be based on a deficient understanding of the nature of political legitimacy: without clearer evidence of a will on the parts of Iraq's multiple peoples to 'brave labour and danger for their liberation', to use J. S. Mill's words, not to mention a well-thought-out plan for securing it, the project was doomed to cause a violent breakdown in such order as Iraqis enjoyed (Mill 1984 [1859]: 122). These were the reasons why I joined the demonstrations in Dublin, where I lived at that time.

But I was also frustrated at the message expressed by some of my fellow protesters – a message that many who protest nowadays continue to carry forward. They weren't only marching against this particular war. Their protest was against war in general. By contrast, I wasn't convinced that pacifism offered the best starting point for debating a case like the Iraq invasion. Pacifists have a steep hill to climb in order to persuade others that war in any particular case is unjustified. To succeed, first they have to persuade people of something that's very hard to prove: that war can *never* be justified. That 'never' might literally mean *ever*: neither in the present circumstances of world politics, nor during any other era of human history. Or it might be limited to the era of total war, of nuclear arms, of 'new wars', or of whatever it might be: 'never' might mean 'in none of the cases we are likely to face in the foreseeable future'. But either way, I believe that most of the people that protesters seek to engage will be convinced to begin with that war *is* justifiable in at least some imaginable cases, however peculiar or extreme. In particular, they are likely to believe that a world that continues to resemble in any essential respects the world of the 1920s and 1930s cannot rule out a priori the possibility of a just war.

What I will call 'the just war idea' – the belief that war is sometimes justifiable, provided it is initiated in the right circumstances and conducted and concluded in the right way – is, as many might think nowadays, part of our global 'common sense'. It contributes to what Michael Walzer called 'the ordinary language in which we argue about particular wars, whether we speak as political representatives, journalists, academics, or simply as citizens' (2004: x). But the idea has been criticized. Not only do pacifists raise doubts about it, but so too do some who argue from a sharply contrasting position: realists in foreign policy sometimes question the plausibility of trying to apply moral principles in war and contemporary international politics more generally.

Some criticize the just war idea in another way. They maintain that just war theory helps license aggression and neo-colonial adventurism by offering the leaders of powerful states a ready-made rhetoric of public justification.[1] This may be true, but the position for which I will argue is that just war theory is also an indispensable tool for criticizing those who promote war. As long as world politics holds up the possibility – however infrequent – that war may occasionally be morally necessary, then we will continue to need just war theory to guide debate and action in contemporary politics. That way, when some state or other organization makes a bogus claim to have justification for resorting to arms, as will inevitably and all too commonly be the case, the best critical reply will be to argue, not that war is never justifiable, but that *this* war is unjustified because it fails by the standards of the just war idea.

Preface

Instead of arguing from a pacifist position, then, it seems to me that the best way to debate the justifications offered for war, first in Iraq, and then in the various other cases over the years since 2003, was on the basis of what will be common ground for many people: the belief that, as it were, 'just war' *is* possible, at least in principle. Each particular case ought to be debated in light of that possibility: is it a case that satisfies the necessary criteria of a just war? Or is it not? In this way, we can debate wars in prospect, as when people asked in 2015 and 2018 should the United Kingdom join the United States in bombing Syria (or, as it might be, in attacking North Korea or Iran)? We can debate the justification and the conduct of a war as it unfolds. And then we can debate it in retrospect.

To make the case that just war is possible, I argue that we need to rethink the terms in which the very idea of a just war is understood. First, we need to recognize that just war theory is as much about justifying war as it is about restricting it and restraining those who participate in it. Second, I think we need to recognize greater affinities between just war theory and contributions to political ethics that are more often identified with 'realism'. The vitally important moral limits on human action that just war theory is built around, particularly in its contemporary, liberal form, have to be seen as part of a wider theory that seeks to achieve the best possible balance between moral restraint and moral necessity. For those in positions of political leadership – whether as presidents and prime ministers or as revolutionaries and rebels – these may be characterized using Max Weber's terms by way of a contrast between moral conviction and political responsibility. But I also want to emphasize the affinity between just war theory at its most basic level of commitment and some varieties of what's known as 'contingent' pacifism.

In chapter 1, I sketch the historical origins of the just war idea and review some lines of division between different contemporary schools of just war thinking. I then turn in chapter 2 to a key question: what else do you have to believe in order to believe that just war is possible? Answering it clarifies just what it is that we need to defend if we are to provide sufficient grounds for believing that just war is possible. I argue that the just war idea relies on a set of basic convictions and assumptions that are both prima facie plausible and likely to be shared even by many people who wouldn't think of themselves as followers of just war theory.

I then respond to a series of possible objections to these beliefs and, hence, to the possibility of just war. Chapter 3 focuses on problems with what just war theorists nowadays call the *jus ad bellum* (that part of the theory that concerns the justice of going to war), and chapter 4, on the idea of a *jus in bello* (the theory of right conduct *in* war) and the compromises that might be necessary in concluding otherwise just wars (questions of *jus post bellum*). In the course of my defence, I build up an interpretation of the just war idea that resists both overly formal and excessively idealistic approaches to the question. My claim is ultimately that just war is possible if it means *war that is all-things-considered justifiable in the circumstances*. This requires taking account of the inevitability of error, compromise and human failure. A possible just war is ultimately one that is less evil than the evil it resists, even if this typically means falling some way short of the 'ideal' image of just war envisaged in theory.

Acknowledgements

I have incurred a number of debts while working on this book and would like to express my gratitude to some people and institutions that helped along the way. George Owers commissioned it and has proven an extraordinarily thorough and perceptive editor since, providing excellent guidance at all stages of the work. I am grateful to George, to David Held and to two anonymous referees for reading the entire draft and offering comments. I completed it during my first three months at the University of Durham. I would like to thank my new colleagues at the School of Government and International Affairs, and especially John Williams, Head of School, for providing such a welcoming and collegial environment in which to work. Many thanks to Maria Dimova-Cookson and Beth Kahn for discussing my ideas for the book over lunch on a number of occasions. I am grateful to Julia Davies and Rachel Moore for editorial support at Polity and to Gail Ferguson for copy-editing the final manuscript with such care. I would like to thank the Leverhulme Trust for its generous support. Much-needed time during which to complete the manuscript was provided by a Leverhulme Major Research Fellowship. Finally, I dedicate this book to my parents, David and Gladys Finlay, to say thanks for their love and many, many kindnesses.

1

Ideas and Ideals of the Just War

And over time, as codes of law sought to control violence within groups, so did philosophers and clerics and statesmen seek to regulate the destructive power of war. The concept of a 'just war' emerged, suggesting that war is justified only when certain conditions were met . . .

Barack Obama,
Nobel Peace Prize Speech (2009)

When he accepted the Nobel Peace Prize in 2009, Barack Obama's speech raised some eyebrows. Rather than speaking purely of the need for peace, he spoke of war and how it might sometimes be 'justified'. It had to meet certain conditions: it must be 'waged as a last resort or in self-defense'; the 'force used' must be 'proportional' and civilians must be 'spared from violence' but, notably, only 'whenever possible' (Obama 2009). The speech alludes, then, to a practice of war that is limited in its occasions, its aims and its methods. But, even so, the award was for contributing to world peace (for *the most or the best work for fraternity between nations, the abolition or reduction of standing armies and for the holding and promotion of peace congresses'*). So why reference the idea of a 'just war' when accepting it?

I think the reason is likely to have been the fact that he did so as a new head of state – and not just of *any* state: Obama was a newly minted president of the United States of America. As such, he was aware that, even with the best will in the world, he wouldn't be permitted in the coming years to avoid being implicated in bloodshed and the prosecution of war. ('I am the commander-in-chief of the military of a nation in the midst of two wars.') Obama therefore had to accept the wisdom offered by Max Weber in his essay 'Politics as a Vocation': politicians may have deep and strong convictions, including a commitment to peace and a preference for non-violence; but their role as heads of state commits them equally to wielding the sword where needed. The ethics that might seem to arise directly from their deepest convictions must therefore find a way to live alongside the demands of political responsibility (Weber 2004 [1919]: 83–4). And the ethics of responsibility demand the resort to violence to defend the innocent, to maintain state security and to uphold order in the world. Given the possibility that these two demands are likely to conflict, what is a political leader to do?

Obama's speech steers a well-travelled course between two extremes. On one side extends the path of so-called 'realists' who claim descent from Niccolò Machiavelli and his advice to the new prince: do 'the right thing' when you can, but recognize that politics requires doing wrong when you must (Machiavelli 1998: 61). Morals, on this view, have very limited scope in politics: effective political leadership demands that they be suspended in order to focus on doing what is necessary and effective. On the other side lies the path of what Jean Bethke Elshtain calls 'the beautiful souls' (following Hegel): those who would let the heavens fall rather than sully themselves by engaging in armed force (1982: 341–2).

Both views, in fact, agree that resorting to force is inherently wrong (even if Machiavellians counsel doing it anyway). But Obama's speech references a third perspective, which holds that resorting to force in appropriate circumstances is *not* morally wrong. It doesn't dirty the hands of the politician when it is constrained by rules that define both the proper occasions for its use and the moral limits that those engaging in it should observe. This, in a nutshell, is the 'just war' idea. It rejects the doctrine of *raison d'état*, according to which violence may be used when it is to the advantage of the state. But it also denies the idea that violence, and war especially, are unjustifiable. Following St Augustine, it holds that there are sometimes worse things than war and that peace should not be bought at the cost of at least some kinds of profound injustice (Rengger 2013: 47).

So Obama accepts an award for contributing to world peace but argues that peace demands a practice falling somewhere between pacifism and realism, one that borrows some wisdom from both. A truly principled commitment to peace, he implies, demands a willingness to resort to war when necessary as a means of securing it. The aim of this short book is to ask whether, in fact, the synthesis of realism and the commitment to peace is credible: is just war possible? Can the demands of moral principle and political responsibility be reconciled along the lines outlined by Obama? My view is that they can, but in order to persuade anyone of this, it is necessary to defend the possibility of a just war from a variety of doubts that might be expressed about it.

Before we do, let's turn to a crucial, basic question: what does the just war idea consist of? What are its essential components?

1.1 Origins and sources

One way to answer these questions is to draw on the history of ideas and argue that just war theory is essentially a *tradition*. As such, its constituents are found in a canon of historical texts dating back to the classical Greeks and Romans (Johnson 1975, 1981).

Much of the terminology and intellectual equipment of current just war thinking can, in fact, be traced back to much older sources. 'Wars,' wrote the Roman orator and philosopher Cicero, 'ought not to be undertaken except for this purpose, that we may live in peace, without injustice; and once victory has been secured, those who were not cruel or savage in warfare should be spared' (quoted in Neff 2005: 13). His declaration encapsulates the two dimensions of just war theory that would be most fully developed in centuries to come, the idea of a *jus ad bellum* and that of a *jus in bello*.

The theory of the just war flourished at the hands of Christian theologians and lawyers in Europe from the period of late Roman antiquity right up to the early-modern era (Bellamy 2006; Brunstetter and O'Driscoll 2017; Johnson 1975). Theologians such as St Augustine and St Thomas Aquinas contributed to a theory according to which the seemingly pacifist tendencies in Christian doctrine could be reconciled with the responsibility of political rulers to defend the innocent and challenge injustice.

Medieval theorists generally thought of restraint *in* war (*jus in bello*) from the perspective of those who fought with just cause rather than as a matter that had a bearing on both sides in a just war. Their emphasis on acting out of love and a desire for justice, which together could justify killing those who perpetrated wrongs, meant that it was hard to see how those fighting *against* a just war could be justified in killing. It was therefore extremely important for the development of a characteristically modern theory when the Catholic philosopher and theologian Francisco de Vitoria introduced the idea of 'simultaneous ostensible justice' (Johnson 1975: 20). In his lectures on war at the University of Salamanca in the 1530s, he argued that war might be justified – in a limited sense – on *both* sides in some cases. Even if *you* had a truly just cause (objectively), your opponents might have a reasonable belief that they did too, albeit that it was based in 'invincible error' (Vitoria 1991 [1539]: 312–13, but cf. 306–7 [§20]). And if this was possible, then the reverse might be possible, too: it might turn out, in hindsight, that you were the ones with the error. If so, then it behoves all fighting even in ostensibly just wars to be modest and restrained rather than self-righteous and fanatical in the pursuit of their goals (Johnson 1975: 20).

With this highly influential move, Vitoria contributed to a current in modern thought in which the idea of a substantive *jus ad bellum* – a claim to have the moral right to wage war in the face of injustice – increasingly fell into the background. The early modern period saw the focus of inquiry shift increasingly onto the *jus in bello* and the possibility of upholding a form of international law that would be agnostic about which sides had just cause, applying equally to all. This idea culminated in the work of Enlightenment theorists, Christian Wolff and Emer de Vattel, for whom a legitimate war came to be identified as one that followed an appropriate formal set of rules (*guerre reglé* or 'regular war').[1]

As a result of these developments, the classic doctrine inherited from medieval just war theory declined after the seventeenth century. By the nineteenth, states would increasingly come to view the recourse to war as an option to be decided upon based on political expediency and the pursuit of the national interest (Walzer 1977: 63). But this more permissive view of war was in turn eclipsed with the revival of just war theory in the twentieth century.

1.2 Contemporary theories

When it was focused chiefly on the *jus in bello*, modern international law diverged from the just war idea in an important sense by pushing questions of *jus ad bellum* into the background. But as James Turner Johnson argues, international law is itself descended from the just war tradition, particularly through the seminal influence of Hugo Grotius's early seventeenth-century 'reframing' of its ideas (Johnson 2013: 26).

By the mid-twentieth century, the increasingly elaborate legal codes of *jus in bello* would be counterbalanced by what was in effect a legal *jus ad bellum*, thus establishing a closer alignment between international law and a version of the just war idea. Building on foundations laid by the Kellogg–Briand Pact of 1928, the Charter of the United Nations, which came into force in 1945, enshrines two principles that can be interpreted in a way that resonates with the just war tradition. First, it outlaws the use of warfare as a means of mutual threat for purposes of purely national self-interest (Article 2[4]). Second, it also identifies limited cases in which a resort to armed force may be justified. The UN Security Council has the authority to use military force in response to sufficiently serious threats to international peace and security (UN Charter, Ch. VII). And states faced with imminent threat may resort to war if necessary to protect themselves, pending action by the UN (Article 51 of the UN Charter).

Interpreted in this way, the UN Charter sets out a template for justified war whose most famous philosophical proponent is Michael Walzer. Walzer characterizes the view it expresses as that of the 'legalist paradigm'. States interact with each other much like individuals in domestic society. Both are subject to rules prohibiting mutual aggression. And both have rights of self-defence when faced with wrongful threats and are permitted to use force – even lethal violence – if doing so is the only way to meet such threats. Thus far, the argument is based on analogy: as long as states internationally have enough significant features in common with individuals domestically, we might view them as being able to claim the right to similar sorts of action and to be able to offer similar reasons for doing so. An additional reason, however, for granting states the right to wage war in the face of aggression is that, '[i]n the absence of an universal state, men and women are protected and their interests represented only by their own governments'. With some significant exceptions, individuals therefore have a profound stake in defending their states from threats (Walzer 1977: 51–63, 86–108; cf. Rawls 1999: 79–80, 89–93).

On the Walzerian view, then, states are the key agents in just war theory. They are central to the way 'just cause' is defined, and it is chiefly their governments that have the authority to declare war. This, we might say, is the first dimension of the 'orthodox' view that Walzer has come to be identified with. A second is found in Walzer's account of *jus in bello* which, like his *jus ad bellum*, corresponds in its essential features quite closely to contemporary international law.

All modern views on *jus in bello* share a commitment to two core principles, discrimination and proportionality. Where they differ is in how these principles should be interpreted. Walzer's view is built around a doctrine of 'the moral equality of soldiers', according to which all legitimate combatants have the same rights, privileges and duties. This is true regardless of whether or not the war in which they fight satisfies the conditions of *jus ad bellum* (1977: 34–44). So, in the Second World War, for instance, whether someone fought as a British army conscript or as a volunteer in the Wehrmacht, the same rules applied. Provided they abided by the *jus in bello,* both had prisoner-of-war status if captured and immunity from prosecution for fighting. And they had what's sometimes called a 'privilege' of attacking enemy combatants, which they could claim even if doing so was likely to harm civilians collaterally. Both also had a duty to respect the immunity of non-combatants. This duty is serious and onerous: when doing so is necessary to minimize risks to civilians, soldiers, Walzer emphasizes, are under a duty to accept greater risks to themselves. It is not sufficient merely *not to intend harm* to civilians; they have to *intend not to harm* them. And any harms thus caused shouldn't be disproportionate to the value of the soldiers' military objectives (Walzer 1977: 151–6).

This account of the morality of *jus in bello* corresponds closely to the basic principles of contemporary international law. Just as Walzer argues that the moral principles of *jus in bello* are independent of those of the *jus ad bellum,* the Law of Armed Conflict (LOAC) is agnostic so far as the causes of war are concerned: all participants are treated the same. The consensus between moral theory and international law has lately been challenged, however, by a series of increasingly influential 'revisionist' philosophers.[2] Their motivation may be traced back to moral commitments which have more in common with human rights than with either the UN Charter or the LOAC.

The most influential revisionists all take the value and rights of the individual person to be the bedrock of moral analysis and are apt to question any assertion of values not reducible entirely to the value of lives lived by individual people (Rodin 2002: 143). As such, these philosophers might all be characterized as 'cosmopolitan' (Coady 2008; Fabre 2012; McMahan 2009; only Cécile Fabre has offered an account of just war systematically articulated through a wider cosmopolitan political theory). Revisionists place less emphasis than Walzer does on the significance of political community and tend to disagree quite strongly with any suggestion that the morality of war is irreducibly collective in nature. Let's take three of the most dramatic challenges in turn.

The belief that nations generally have a moral right of self-defence has been the subject of controversy during the past couple of decades. The challenge was laid down by Richard Norman (1995) and David Rodin (2002). If the ultimate values in global politics are individuals, then why should we assume that *states* are the subjects of defensive rights in war? Are the two ideas – individual and national rights of self-defence – not likely to point in opposite directions in some cases?

If we maintain national defence as the major, paradigmatic principle of just war and international order, it potentially gives rise to two sorts of problem. On the one hand, it might lead us to prohibit some of the wars that just war theory ought to endorse: the right of each nation to defend itself is at odds with the right of another nation to send soldiers into its territory against its will in a justified humanitarian intervention. But, on the other hand, the national defence principle also seems likely to permit wars that it is hard to justify morally. Citing a principle of national defence in support of a war to protect uninhabited territory or in support even of national independence when faced with an aggressor that doesn't threaten any reduction in human rights protections raises difficult questions about what values are actually being protected (Rodin 2002: 132, 148–9). If the values of territorial integrity or national independence as such are worth killing for – and in particular, engaging in forms of warfare that will inevitably result in the deaths of many *innocent* people as bystanders – then we need an account of why they are. And if they are not, then we would need some other account of why wars of national defence are justified in such cases.[3]

The commitment to individual rights as ultimate values seems, then, to be in tension at certain points with a principle of national defence. But the problems don't stop with the orthodox account of *jus ad bellum*. Analysis of war in individualist terms is also at odds, Jeff McMahan has argued, with the doctrine of moral equality and the orthodox *jus in bello*. Let's think again about analogies: individuals are widely assumed to have a right of self-defence that is triggered when other people wrongfully threaten them and leave them with no other choice but to resort to force. When this happens, do we think that the right to use force is *symmetrical*? That is, do *both* parties have the same right at this point, the attacker *and* her victim? Most people would be inclined to think not: justified defence by the victim doesn't trigger a reciprocal right of self-defence on the part of her attacker. Analogously, when one state fights defensively against wrongful aggression by another, we don't assume that the aggressor can claim a right of self-defence against its victim *while aggressing*. So why is it, then, that we think in such a radically different way when it comes to individual combatants fighting in just wars? Why don't we regard soldiers fighting on behalf of the victims of international aggression as exercising defensive rights and view their opponents as individual wrongdoers by virtue of the part they play in an act of collective aggression?

McMahan has led a scholarly onslaught against the orthodox view on this score. He maintains that none of the arguments on offer provide a satisfy-ing explanation of the widely held assumption that 'unjust warriors' are justified in fighting and have the same combat rights as their opponents (McMahan 2009). Opposing combatants in a just war are not generally moral equals – even if, perhaps for good reason, they are conventionally granted the status of legal equals. Followers of both Walzer and McMahan might agree that all soldiers ought to follow the LOAC *and* that all should be immune from prosecution as long as they do so. So the two approaches won't necessarily give rise to radically divergent practices of warfare. But there is nevertheless fundamental disagreement between them at a deeper level of analysis and interpretation (see Finlay 2017a: 75–7; and passim on popular representations of the tension between these views).

Finally, Cécile Fabre offers, among much else, a challenge to the principle of legitimate authority (Fabre 2008, 2012; see also Steinhoff 2007: ch. 1). The traditional view in just war theory held until very recently that 'war,' properly speaking, was a condition that only occurred between public authorities with a legitimate claim to represent the common good of their subjects. States were generally viewed, therefore, as the only entities with authority to wage war. During the modern period, this view came under pressure as the need to bring non-state belligerents under the regulation of the law of war became increasingly urgent. Fabre challenges not only the traditional, state-centred view but also a revised view according to which non-state sides need to demonstrate political legitimacy in order to justify waging war. On her account, the right that an individual may claim to defence of her own person and basic interests is sufficiently weighty that she may not be deprived of it by the mere fact that she cannot do so under the authority of a legitimate political leadership. Any individual or group of individuals may therefore initiate something we might call 'war' in case of imminent threat to their basic rights, regardless of whether a 'legitimate authority' exists to lead them (Fabre 2008; Reitberger 2013; cf. Finlay 2010; Parry 2017).

1.3 A vibrant field of debate

We hear constant references to '*the* just war tradition', '*the* theory of the just war' and even to '*the* just war doctrine', expressions that suggest some degree of unison among thinkers (e.g. BBC 2014). And yet, as we can see, there is wide disagreement between different proponents of the just war (Lang 2016: 289–90; though cf. McMahan 2007: 669). If just war theorists cannot agree amongst themselves, we might worry, how can we expect them to establish a univocal position attractive enough to persuade doubters about the feasibility of just war?

In the next chapter, I'm going to highlight something much deeper that people who subscribe to the idea of a just war share. But before I do, let's look at some common commitments in the field even at surface level. By and large, all the contemporary theorists mentioned so far agree on the primacy of human individuals, on the importance of their most fundamental interests and on the idea that they ought to be protected as rights. Moreover, these rights include not only private goods but also goods pursued through social interaction and collective, sometimes political, activity (i.e. collective self-determination). Orthodox theorists and revisionists alike agree that respect for individuals therefore requires that their collective projects and institutions be supported and protected. And this means that protecting the freedom of states and other political institutions might sometimes be legitimate causes for war (Fabre 2012; Rawls 1999; Walzer 1977).

The emphasis on individual rights is also reflected in the common ground shared by theorists in debating the *jus in bello*. Even if McMahan differs from Walzer and other orthodox theorists like Yitzhak Benbaji (2008, 2009, 2011) or Seth Lazar (2015) on the underlying 'deep' morality of war, all agree that the LOAC ought to be followed in most circumstances (cf. Haque 2017). And when revisionists argue that there are exceptions to the rule of noncombatant immunity, they don't really depart from Walzer, who conceded as much in *Just and Unjust Wars* (cf. Fabre 2012: 242–56; Finlay 2015: 219–85; McMahan 2009: 203–35 with Rawls 1999: 98–9 and Walzer 1977: 251–68; 2004: 33–50).

The disagreements between theories about important issues in the analysis and interpretation of the ethics of war are significant. But they are probably no more than we would expect in a vibrant field of moral debate. There is, in any case, an underlying set of beliefs which, as I'll now argue, constitute the basic credo of those who feel compelled to accept the just war idea in some form.

2

The Just War Creed

So, just war theory is flourishing as a field of contemporary political theory. But as we saw at the outset, there are many sceptics who doubt the possibility of a just war for one reason or another. How can it be defended?

To do so, it is necessary to simplify things by zoning in on the bare essentials. These are twofold. First, we need to know what the most basic convictions are that just war theorists share across the various contemporary divisions (orthodox versus revisionist, religious versus secular, and so on): we need to ask what are the core convictions that define someone as a just war theorist? And, second, we need to specify why just war theorists think these beliefs are true: what background assumptions do the core convictions of just war theory depend on?

If we can specify both – the core convictions and the assumptions that support them – then we will know what it is that really *must* be defended if we are to answer 'yes' to the question in the title of this book.

2.1 Core convictions

Even when they differ about many other things, most contemporary just war theorists share three generic beliefs about war and morality. The first (I) is that war is a great evil that should be avoided in all but the most exceptional circumstances. Whether this 'moral presumption against war' was upheld by the major Christian thinkers earlier in the tradition is disputed (compare Johnson's rejection of the idea [1999: 35–6] with Coates's restatement of the conventional wisdom [2008: 190]). But it is widely accepted that the justifications for war offered by Augustine, Aquinas and others were argued through dialogue with a pacifist alternative (Reichberg 2008: 12–14). In any case, the presumption has generally come to be seen as axiomatic during the post-Second World War era, both among theorists and more widely in the mind of the general public (Holmes 2017: 27–8). The presumption against war is stated as a basic starting point in the Pastoral Letter from the US National Conference of Catholic Bishops, 'The Challenge of Peace' (1983; see also Childress 1978; for a Protestant perspective, see Biggar 2013a: 8). In secular just war theory, as we have seen, Walzer adopted a view on *jus ad bellum* that harmonized with the legal presumption against war established by international law (1977: 62, 107; cf. 2004: 88–9; also May 2008: 5–6, 103, 105, 339). And even if its proponents are sometimes willing to justify a larger number of different types of war, we can say the same thing of revisionism as Tony Coady says of just war theory in general: '[it] is there to tell us not to engage in war unless certain hard-to-satisfy conditions are met' (Coady 2008: 15–16; McMahan 2009: 150).

The second conviction, however, is that (II) war might nevertheless be justified when faced with great evils of certain types. There are, in other words, exceptions to the general presumption against war, however rare and narrowly defined. Which evils precisely might trigger an exception varies between different schools of thought, but the underlying conviction is the same for just war theory across the board.

And the third shared conviction is that, even if it is sometimes justified, (III) war ought to be fought with considerable restraint. Restraint might be based on the doctrine of moral equality and international law or on judgements about individual moral responsibility and innocence or on another basis. But whichever way the idea is unpacked, the underlying conviction is that some forms of violence should be regarded as impermissible.

I take these three beliefs to be definitional of the just war idea and the family of theories that uphold it. Individual theorists, of course, always have other beliefs too – concerning the nature of the international order and global justice, or of political authority and the state, or concerning human nature and history, for instance. And they interpret the three convictions in different ways. But in order to claim membership of the just war family, their theories must converge on these three convictions as core beliefs. If someone accepted, say, the first conviction but rejected conviction II (and perhaps even if they accepted some version of III) then they would be more appropriately described as a pacifist, and they certainly wouldn't believe that 'just war' is a real moral possibility. Likewise, even if they accepted III and thought that war was justifiable, they wouldn't really be committed to just war theory if they rejected I: the profile of their moral convictions about war would fit the view that sees states as having a right to resort to war as a means of securing their interests in general, rather than only as a means of responding to grave injustices and as a matter of urgent necessity.

But there is even more to the basic core of just war theory, or so I would like to argue. If your view on war is built around these three beliefs, then I think it means that another, deeper and simpler set of assumptions is at work in the background: these are the underlying assumptions on the basis of which someone might arrive at the three core convictions. So if we can find reasons to accept the underlying assumptions, then we too are likely to find the three convictions of just war theory persuasive – and to believe that just war *is* possible. In fact, I suspect many readers will already have come to accept these assumptions.

2.2 Underlying assumptions

The background assumptions that support the just war idea are more often implicit than explicit, and they might be formulated in a number of different ways. But I think the three core just war convictions are likely to make sense if you also believe the following to be true:

1 that killing is a peculiarly grave prima facie wrong (i.e. there are moral reasons not to kill that are usually compelling);

2 that letting grave injustices such as unjustified killing pass without serious attempts (where possible) to impede or prevent them is wrong;

3 that attempts to perpetrate grave injustices are likely to remain a feature of human history for the foreseeable future (perhaps in perpetuity);

4 that sometimes the only means (or the means with the fewest evil consequences) of impeding or preventing grave injustices threatened by others requires killing;

5 that sometimes the wrong of failing to impede or prevent injustices threatened by others would be greater than the (prima facie) wrong of those killings that impeding or preventing them would require.

Let's run through them in turn.

The words 'prima facie' in assumption 1 reflect the thought that killing is *generally* wrong: wrong, that is, unless special reasons are offered to justify it. The prima facie wrongfulness of deliberate killing is a near-universal moral intuition, enshrined in the ethical codes of many cultures and societies

(Holmes 2017: 27; May 2015: 3; McMahan 2003: 189). The idea that war is impermissible most of the time is grounded on this assumption: this is so because it involves killing as well as wider destruction of the human world. It's worth spelling this out a little more.

War necessarily involves the intentional killing of enemy soldiers. But many soldiers also intentionally kill enemy civilians and others who find themselves rendered vulnerable by the war. When considering the possibility of war, it's wise to presume that 'war crimes' of some sort are highly likely to occur. These crimes wouldn't themselves be justified, of course. But to initiate war is to open Pandora's box, so to speak: it frequently leads to unintended events. And there will be other unintended consequences, too: even soldiers committed to fighting discriminately will sometimes kill ambient non-combatants. What we nowadays call 'collateral damage' is generally assumed to be inevitable. So, by virtue of all these killings – many of which are intended, most of which are foreseeable in one sense or another – there is a strong (but not indefeasible) moral presumption against initiating wars.

But if killing and intentional destruction are great evils when perpetrated for ostensibly good purposes, they are presumably worse (all else being equal) when carried out for wrongful aims. They are often used to serve a variety of unjust purposes: to terrorize or even eliminate minority ethnic groups; to establish tyrannical domination over foreign states; to rob peoples of valuable natural resources; and so on. People who are threatened with wholly unjustified violence suffer not only the risk that they may be murdered or mutilated, but also the indignity of being subjugated, stripped of their autonomy and bent to the arbitrary will of others. Assumption 2 is that those who *could* do something to prevent such injustices have a prima facie duty to do so. It may be that the victims are entitled to do so on their own behalf, in which case perhaps we might say they had a 'right' to defend themselves. But when the injustices are threatened between states or between large groups of people – races, classes, peoples or whatever they may be – then those who are in a position to resist are likely to do so, not only on their own behalf (thereby exercising a right) but also on behalf of other victims in need of assistance. In this case, we might be prepared to say that those who can resist have a duty to protect those who cannot. And so, as assumption 2 states, it would be wrong for those with the capacity to do otherwise to permit such injustices to be perpetrated (see e.g. Walzer 1971: 9).

The third assumption is simple on the face of things but nevertheless disputed, as we'll see in the next chapter: whether by virtue of their beliefs about human nature or their knowledge of past history or theory about future development or for some other reason, I presume most people are unlikely to believe that injustice backed by violence is soon to disappear from the world. So the prima facie duty to resist and assist others in defending themselves is likely to keep recurring for the foreseeable future. Well, this assumption is axiomatic to just war theory.

Then we get to the more controversial claims – where the work of defending the just war idea is hardest. To uphold conviction II, that war is sometimes justifiable as an exception to conviction I, the general rule prohibiting it in most cases, you have to believe two things. First, you would have to believe (assumption 4) that sometimes war is a necessary means of defending against the wrongs that assumption 2 refers to. It is a 'means' if it can be effective in doing so; it is 'necessary' if (roughly speaking) no other means are available or if the effectiveness of all the alternatives is too uncertain or morally costly by comparison. If war is unnecessary in this sense, then it is highly unlikely to be justifiable: alternatives that don't involve systematic killing ought to be attempted. But more than this, for war to be justified, the wrongfulness of permitting others to inflict grave injustice would have to be great enough to outweigh the prima facie wrongs it requires you to perpetrate (reflecting assumption 5).

If (and, I think, only if) you accept all five of these assumptions – or closely related variants of them – then you will also share the three core convictions of just war theory. So, if these assumptions can be convincingly defended, then so can the possibility of a just war – or so I hope to show.

2.3 Conditions of just war: unpacking the assumptions

Just war theory sets out a series of well-known criteria for judging wars. They specify the conditions under which resorting to and fighting a war would be less bad than non-resistance. These provide an architecture within which to frame judgements about whether a particular war satisfied the conditions implicit in assumption 5.

> ### *Jus ad bellum*
>
> i.   Just Cause
> ii.   Legitimate Authority
> iii. Right Intention
> iv. Last Resort (Necessity)
> v.   Proportionality
> vi. Prospect of Success

Just cause, for instance, specifies that war is justified only against threats grave enough to give rise to the duties referred to in assumptions 2 and 5. A substantive account of this criterion would define what exactly those types of threat are: those so serious that the moral urgency of responding to them might override the prima facie duty not to kill. Somewhat more controversially, war is recognized as a legitimate recourse only when undertaken by someone or some people with the right kind of 'authority'. We've seen how some philosophers raise doubts about this principle. I will suggest some reasons why attention to the authority of those leading a war might yet be important.

Right intention is also less prominent nowadays than in medieval theory (though see Grynaviski 2016). Modern, secular accounts of just war have different priorities, giving greater priority to worldly consequences over war's motivation (e.g. Walzer 1977: 101–8). Theorists are generally less worried by the spiritual or moral effects of war on those prosecuting it (though with some exceptions, e.g. Sherman 2005). But they would generally agree with the Christian tradition that if wars are fought for glory or for an escape from the humdrum rhythms of peacetime, then they should be morally condemned. Similarly, while they might think it prudent to accept that ulterior motives could help incentivize engagement in wars that also have humanitarian purposes, they appreciate that such motives detract from the worthiness of fighting them and might undermine just outcomes through conflicts of interest. In any case, the criterion should be taken to assert that war must be intended to discharge the duties indicated by its cause (those indicated by assumption 2).

To be less morally bad than not fighting, war must satisfy three additional conditions, sometimes characterized as 'prudential': (iv) it must be a last resort, which is to say, necessary: there should be no remaining alternatives for addressing the same problems that are less destructive than war; (v) it must be proportionate in terms of the expected balance of costs and gains; and (vi) it must not be futile: it must have a 'reasonable chance of success'. Let's call these the *necessity*, *proportionality* and *success* conditions.

Fairly obviously, assumption 4 and the necessity condition are closely aligned. Both reflect the worries expressed in assumption 1 and conviction I: killing and war are evils that are permissible only when there is no other choice – or, at least, none with comparable prospects, a point I will come back to in chapter 3. Likewise, assumption 5 and *ad bellum* proportionality are close relatives: the proportionality condition reflects an expectation that wars can sometimes be less evil than the threats that non-resistance would allow to happen and permits them only when this is true. The success condition is presupposed by both the necessity and proportionality conditions: neither can be satisfied if there is no chance of success sufficient to render war necessary and then counterbalance its evils.

Jus in bello

1. Discrimination
2. (*in bello*) Proportionality
3. (*in bello*) Necessity

Finally, the core principles of the *jus in bello* help specify more fully those conditions that the prosecution of war generally has to meet in order to satisfy the conditions implied by assumption 5, that the wrong of non-resistance must be greater than the wrong of fighting. If the methods of fighting involve deliberately killing people who are immune from attack (a violation of the principle of discrimination) or the infliction of harms that are unnecessary to the pursuit of military objectives or disproportionate to their value, then war is less likely to satisfy this condition than if it respects their immunity. I will give these issues more detailed attention in chapter 4.

2.4 *Conclusion*

So, in spite of the apparent complexity of the various lists of conditions associated with just war theory and the variety of doctrines espoused by its different proponents, its underlying creed of basic beliefs is relatively simple. They consist of three convictions and these, in turn, are supported by five, relatively straightforward assumptions. If just war is impossible, it will be because one or more of these assumptions is untrue.

3

'Just Cause' and the Possibility of *Jus ad Bellum*

So what objections do just war theory and its underlying assumptions face? Well, the prima facie wrongfulness of killing is widely accepted across a range of religious, political and philosophical traditions. So I think assumption 1 can be taken as read. In which case, just war is most likely to be challenged on the basis of assumptions 2 to 5. To defend the possibility of just war, I shall therefore respond in this chapter and the next to some objections that might seem to pose problems for these assumptions.

First, I'll consider objections that particularly concern *resorting* to war: *jus ad bellum*. If we can't answer them, then the claim that just war is possible won't even get off the ground. But I think we can.

3.1 Jus ad bellum *is* redundant

Let's begin with assumption 3. How might belief in the likelihood of wrongful threats and injustice be cast in doubt?

One such possibility comes from pacifist thought. Dustin Ells Howes, for instance, argues that the history of western political thought is divided between those who think aggression and violence are incorrigible features of the human condition, and those who don't. It comes down to a dispute about 'human possibilities and limitations. Just war theory is the philosophical taproot of the position that human nature necessitates violence and war [. . .] Pacifism's most important [. . .] legacy is to dispute these claims of necessity, not on ethical grounds, but on the basis of a more realistic anthropology.' A more realistic anthropology, Howes suggests, will reflect the fact that human nature is capable of escaping the conditions in which (wrongful) violence occurs (Howes 2015: 379).

It is true that some philosophers have argued from theories about human nature to the conclusion that violence is an inescapable feature of political life. St Augustine's thinking on the effects of sin in secular history is an important source, as are the writings of Machiavelli and Hobbes. It is also true that some recent work in anthropology, psychology and international relations casts doubt on this conclusion, arguing that humanity has been able to curb its aggressive propensities in a seemingly progressive way (Gat 2017; Linklater 2017; Pinker 2012). If violence is on the wane, then does it suggest we should ditch just war theory?

I tend to doubt it. First, even if wrongful threats did decline radically over time, there are no guarantees against backsliding in the long run (Gat 2017: 187–244). But, in any case, the possibility of just war doesn't depend on believing that aggression is a *necessary* and *perpetual* part of life. Even if it could eventually be extinguished, there is little reason to believe that aggression will disappear very soon. Statistics pointing to a decline in violent death since humanity's earliest ages (e.g. Pinker 2012: ch. 5) don't negate the fact that coordinated threats of violence still frequently occur. Inter-state aggression has been less common since the Second World War, but it hasn't entirely disappeared – witness the Russian annexation of the Crimea (Hathaway and Shapiro 2017: on the infrequency of international war, see 309–35; on Crimea, see 309–11). And, anyway, intra-state conflict remains devastatingly common.

What just war theory *necessarily* assumes is that wrongful threats will sometimes occur in the *foreseeable* future. In this regard, it shares some common ground with what's sometimes called 'pacificism'. For pacificists, global peace is an urgent and feasible moral goal. But aggression and other forms of violence that could potentially justify defensive force are still likely to occur in the non-ideal present (Dower 2009: 144–56). Some contingent pacifists might also agree, not only with assumption 3, but even with variants of the other four (cf. e.g. Fiala 2014: section 2.4). Where they might differ from just war theory is in the degree to which they identify with the quest for alternatives to war, doubts about war's effectiveness, scepticism about the goodwill of governments, or a focus on the corrupting effects of institutionalized violence (Fiala 2008; May 2015; Ryan 2018; for a critical overview of pacifism, see Orend 2013: ch. 9).

There is, therefore, little distance separating the just war theorist from many pacifists on the point in question: assumption 3 is reasonably secure, provided we formulate it in a contingent way rather than as a universal truth.

3.2 Jus ad bellum *is* groundless

A second objection takes aim chiefly at the idea that we have moral duties towards others internationally when they need defending. If we didn't and if just war theory relies on the existence of such extensive duties, it might be argued, then it is hard to see how assumption 2 would stand: how could anyone be accused of wrongdoing for failing to assist those threatened with wrongful attack? And if there was no wrong in failing to assist them, then how could failing to fight be morally worse than fighting (assumption 5)? Defeat these two assumptions and the grounds for *jus ad bellum* fail.

This sort of normative scepticism is quite common (Williams 2006: 8, 10) and may be supported by different sorts of background theory. One way is to think with Hobbes, for instance, that you can have duties towards others only when you can carry them out safely. Hobbes thought that there was a high risk of being attacked in any circumstances where people interact without a sovereign to enforce the law between them. But this sort of enforcement occurs only *within* states, he thought, and not over and above them in the international realm. Therefore, the sort of moral duties that assumptions 2 and 5 refer to could only really obligate people interacting within the same state (Hobbes 1996 [1651]; for a critical synopsis of interpretations of Hobbes along these lines, see Malcolm 2002: 432–34).

Another route to similar conclusions might argue from sociability and the foundations of a 'common life'. According to David Hume, for example, principles of justice are established through continuous, repeated social interaction in a political association. Moral duties, then, are essentially social or civic: they have a bearing on the interactions between fellow citizens, compatriots and (in a very immediate sense) neighbours. So while I might have strong obligations towards fellow-citizens as a result of sharing common goals with them, participating in common institutions and engaging in a rich common life, I do not owe them to people outside my community. I might sympathize if I see that they are in need and it may motivate me to help. But this doesn't give rise to *duties as such*, rather to humanitarian impulses and feelings that might lead me to assist them – or not. It's something over which we have greater discretion.[1]

I'll suggest in a moment some reasons why these views about altruistic duties might need correcting. But even if we first of all assumed for the sake of argument that they didn't, the assumptions I sketched out in chapter 2 could still be defended. Sceptical arguments about ethics in *international* affairs still leave room for moral duties in *domestic* politics that could override the duty not to kill, potentially justifying war.

First, sometimes the only hope of protection to be had against a violently oppressive government is if some competent individuals from within the state resist it forcefully. Think, for instance, of internal resistance to fascism during the Second World War – or, more controversially, of the use of force by moderate rebels in the Arab Spring. Both sometimes defended the rights of compatriots from wrongful threats (Manna 2012). Once this sort of internal violence rises above a certain threshold of intensity or organization (on which I'll have more to say in chapter 4), it can be described as civil war. And if it is morally justified, then it would be a *just* civil war (see Buchanan 2013; Fabre 2012: 130–65; Finlay 2015; Parry 2018).

Likewise, second, imagine an internal terrorist insurgency that threatened to replace a state's existing institutions with much more violently oppressive ones. As flawed as it might be, the Iraqi government, for instance, faced such a threat from Daesh ('Islamic State'), especially from 2013 to 2017. So, too, has the Nigerian government from

Boko Haram. I make no claim as to the justness of the methods actually used (see Abdul-Ahad 2017), but in such cases there are at least prima facie moral grounds for armed response and sometimes even for internal warfare.

In the first two types of case, then, fellow citizens are the people to whom defensive duties are owed. And so it already seems possible to speak of just cause for war without defending claims about international duties. But there's yet a further type of case. This is when a government must defend its own people from foreign attack. Justifications for national defence aren't really brought into question by a putatively 'realist' rejection of ethics as a matter between nations. Provided moral duties of assistance and defence are owed between fellow citizens (particularly by citizens in government to those they represent) then assumption 2 holds and assumption 5 might yet turn out to be true.

So, even on the sceptical view, three different kinds of just war could still be possible: revolution, counter-insurgency and national defence. The sorts of just war we'd struggle to explain are those defending *other* states or peoples. Justifying humanitarian interventions or wars to defend other states from aggression within the framework of assumptions set out in chapter 2 depends on a foundation in moral duties owed between citizens or states internationally.

Recently, some theorists have built accounts of just war founded on the claim that people have compelling moral duties towards others simply as fellow human beings and regardless of nationality or borders (see Caney 2005; Fabre 2012, 2016). There isn't the space to offer a philosophical defence of that idea here. But a brief reply to the Hobbesian challenge is that international treaties, intergovernmental institutions and international law have proven much more feasible than it supposes. If trust and cooperation are possible across borders, then it is presumably true that moral duties can extend beyond the state too.

A reply to the argument from 'common life' might challenge its empirical assumptions by pointing out the ways in which globalization, the shared hazards of global warming and environmental damage and the interdependency of peoples in pursuing more widely shared goals have led to a more closely interconnected global experience. If interdependencies and shared values generate duties *within* states, therefore, they must also have that effect *between* them. The thicker the forms of cooperation and mutual understanding, the deeper and richer the forms of common life and mutual moral engagement could be.[2]

In any case, the existence of strong moral duties towards foreign peoples and individuals is widely asserted. The ideas enshrined in the international human rights covenants, as well as in legal commitments to self-determination and non-aggression internationally, all express the idea that there surely must be compelling moral obligations that disregard borders. If this is something readers are committed to, whether on the basis that such rights have a standing in positive international law or on a deeper philosophical basis (see Nickel 2017), then they are likely to accept that the reach of the just war idea extends further to encompass things like humanitarian intervention.

3.3 Jus ad bellum *is* self-defeating

A third challenge claims that the very notion of *jus ad bellum* is incompatible with containing the destructiveness of war. So if the aims of justified war are generally in some sense *humanitarian* then *jus ad bellum* is self-defeating.

The German jurist Carl Schmitt set out an argument along these lines in reaction to what he called

'the discriminating concept of war' after the First
World War (Schmitt 2011 [1937]). The punishment
of Germany by the Versailles Treaty reintroduced,
he thought, the medieval idea that it was possible to
discriminate between just and unjust wars. It was
then reinforced by the Kellogg–Briand Pact, which
outlawed war in 1928, the League of Nations and
the Nuremberg Tribunals. Schmitt's criticism of this
development is set out through a reinterpretation of
the *Jus Publicum Europaeum* that, he argued, had
evolved as a response to the wars of religion in the
sixteenth and early seventeenth centuries. Its central
feature was the 'bracketing' of war by a cluster of
conventional limits and distinctions (Slomp 2005,
2006).

Under this legal order, each war was limited
to a specific geographic location and to formally
acknowledged enemies. Third parties could claim
neutrality, which prevented war from leaching out-
wards and drawing in other states. War had a
definite beginning announced by formal declaration
and a conclusion marked by formal ceasefire and
peace agreements, not by the total defeat of one side
by the other. A formal state of war was recognized
when it had been declared by competent public
authorities; armed conflicts instigated by non-
state parties were mere criminality. Personnel were

distinguished clearly as combatants, liable to attack by their enemies and permitted to attack them in return. Non-combatants were excluded from participation and targeting. Above all, opponents recognized each other as 'conventional' enemies, their relations defined by the formalities of war and not by moral judgements (as the righteous versus the guilty) (Slomp 2005: 508–10).

In effect, this idea of 'regular war' distinguished sharply between *jus in bello* principles and the ends of war by sidelining or, as Schmitt thought, eliminating entirely any meaningful consideration of just cause. A just war was a war conducted according to appropriate *in bello* rules. As such, regular combatants who observed the conventional rules while fighting under orders from their respective governments were entitled to privileged treatment if captured and to immunity from any question of guilt *post bellum*. Likewise, the temptation to attack civilians was diminished by ensuring that winning the war wasn't seen as something commanded by God or by justice as such, and that the enemy wasn't morally demonized. To lose a war, in this framework, was merely to suffer setbacks in the pursuit of state policy, not to let evil defeat righteousness. At least from a cosmic perspective, it was no big deal.

Although motivated by a 'humanitarian' aim, this view of war offered a form of *ad bellum* realism. It purchased *in bello* restraint at the cost of rejecting the possibility of discriminating between justified and unjustified wars. Or at least this is how Schmitt argued.[3] If *ad bellum* discrimination was reintroduced, he thought, warriors would generally presume they were in the right and treat their opponents as 'foes' in an absolute sense, agents of evil who must be vanquished at all costs. Soldiers animated by this belief were unlikely to conclude wars through negotiation: abject surrender by the enemy was the only acceptable conclusion, so wars were likely to be prolonged. And it was hard to see how other states could claim rights of neutrality in a fight between moral right and wrong – discrimination therefore threatened to expand local wars to a global scale.

If Schmitt is right, then just war is impossible in the specific sense set out in chapter 2. To satisfy conviction III, concerning restraint, it would be necessary to abandon conviction II, concerning the justification of war in exceptional cases. But the effect of doing so would not be prohibitive, ruling out such wars. It is permissive: eliminating II entails also having to reject conviction I. In the normative framework outlined by Schmitt, there is no presumption against war. War has to be regarded as a permissible means of pursuing state policy based on the judgement of each nation about what its fundamental interests require.

Defeating conviction II undermines conviction I because any attempt to prohibit war seems likely, as Schmitt feared, to reintroduce the discriminating concept of war by the back door. Consider the steps: war is outlawed, so it becomes a crime; but, if it is a crime to attack another state, then surely the victim must be permitted to defend itself. Then, by outlawing war, we find ourselves back with a variant of conviction II once again: (defensive) war is sometimes permissible as an exception to the general rule (conviction I) (see Hathaway and Shapiro 2017: 9 and 126–7 on the Kellogg–Briand Pact; on the UN Charter, see May 2008: 9–11).

But if this line of thinking is correct, then it also suggests a way of replying and defending the just war idea. The robust *jus in bello* is purchased in Schmitt's account by conceding what Gabriella Slomp calls 'a juridical ... right to wage war ... for every political entity' (Slomp 2006: 441). This is surely far too relaxed as a view of the right to start wars – *restrained* wars, it suggests, are achieved by permitting many *more* wars. We might imagine that wars could still be restricted in this view to those which states deem to be 'necessary' in some non-moral sense. But this is unlikely to mitigate the effects of removing the moral restriction on aggression. 'Necessity,' as Hannah Arendt writes,

> since the time of Livy and through the centuries, has meant many things that we today would find quite sufficient to dub a war unjust rather than just. Conquest, expansion, defence of vested interests, conservation of power in view of the rise of new and threatening powers, or support of a given power equilibrium – all these well-known realities of power politics were not only actually the causes of the outbreak of most wars in history, they were also recognized as 'necessities', that is, as legitimate motives to invoke a decision by arms. (Arendt 2006 [1965]: 3)

As defined by state interests, 'necessity' is almost infinitely permissive.

So, even if the customs and laws of war did bind combatants more successfully when they fought in the more formalized, non-moral practice of war that Schmitt defended, the gains in humanity *in bello* still appear to come at too high a price. This was clear after the First World War demonstrated how 'horribly destructive . . . warfare under conditions of modern technology' could be. The experience prompted the outlawing of war *ad bellum* and, with it, the re-emergence of the discriminating concept of war (Arendt 2006 [1965]: 3).

By the middle of the twentieth century, the horse had already bolted and Schmitt's vision of international legal order was already an exercise in nostalgia. In any case, the development of the modern *jus in bello* is likely to have been caused by multiple factors, as Slomp argues (2006: 441–2) and not solely by the sidelining of just cause. Moreover, even if it was less prominent during the nineteenth century, the idea of a moral *jus ad bellum* continued to influence opinion and shape attitudes towards fighting (e.g. Walzer 1977: 63–4; Witt 2012: 218). The just war idea has always been first and foremost a moral notion that may be contradicted by legal conventions but is unlikely to be extinguished by them. So it's not absolutely clear that the return of the discriminating concept of war rendered the *jus in bello* any more precarious than it had already been.

3.4 Jus ad bellum *is* impossible to satisfy

Let's assume, then, that the objections considered so far can be answered. There is a compelling duty to defend those under threat where possible, whether fellow citizens or foreigners. So, while killing is a prima facie wrong, it is also wrong to stand by idly while they suffer grievous but preventable rights violations (assumption 2). And these sorts of threat are enduring features of human history and likely to persist at least for now (assumption 3). This will take us closer to the goal of defending just war. But what we now need to ask is whether any real war could ever satisfy the conditions of *jus ad bellum* and the assumptions it rests on – in particular assumption 4, that killing is sometimes *necessary* to defeat grave injustices, and 5, that it is sometimes less bad morally to resist by means of war than not to resist.

3.4.1 War is always unnecessary

If we are to persuade people that assumption 4 is reasonable, we need to spell out more fully what it really means for war to be 'necessary'. The first component of necessity in this sense is the possibility of *success*: it's hard to see how war could be seen as *necessary* for some purpose if it has no chance of securing that purpose (Statman 2008: 663).

I presume the belief that a war can sometimes succeed in securing goals is true and likely to be relatively uncontroversial (it is also borne out by some of the examples I'll mention below). But let's review one possible objection. In a recent documentary about the Vietnam War, a veteran of the North Vietnamese army, Bao Ninh, challenged the very idea of speaking of war in terms of success and failure: 'It has been forty years. Even the Vietnamese veterans, we avoid talking about the war. People sing about victory, about liberation. They're wrong. Who won and who lost is not a question. In war, no one wins or loses. There is only destruction. Only those who have never fought like to argue about who won and who lost' (in Burns and Novick 2017: episode 1).

Bao Ninh highlights how the destructiveness of war may be such that all talk of victory, of the attainment of goals such as liberation and, hence, of success or failure, seems beside the point when faced with the experience of war and its aftermath. As Kenneth Waltz once wrote, to ask who won any war is 'like asking who won the San Francisco earthquake' (1959: 1). If correct, then this suggests war cannot satisfy the success condition and so assumption 4 would be refuted. So it's worth probing a little further.

In fact, I think this is the wrong conclusion to draw from Bao Ninh's remarks. Even if we doubted that war by the Vietnamese truly liberated those it subjected to communist government, it is clear that it *had* succeeded in important respects. Indochina saw one of the most famous *military* successes in history when Vo Nguyen Giap's guerrillas routed the forces of the French empire at Dien Bien Phu in 1954. And the traumatic effects of military failure and defeat on the United States since it withdrew in 1975 were surely the result of a certain kind of military and, arguably, political success in resisting its military. Bao Ninh spoke the words above in full awareness of these facts. What he therefore meant isn't that victory in a strategic, military sense was impossible, or even that the political goals of war weren't achieved. It was that they were insufficiently valuable to justify the price paid for them. Something in the nature of war as it is actually experienced means that it just isn't worth it: war, in other words, fails by the test of proportionality. So even if you 'win', in a purely military sense, 'the fruits of victory would be ashes in [your] mouths', as John F. Kennedy put it.

Bao Ninh's doubts – like those alluded to by Waltz – are therefore really about assumption 5 rather than 4. They therefore leave standing the possibility that wars can sometimes *succeed* in a fairly basic sense. But to say that war is *necessary* for certain moral purposes also requires something else: it must offer the best balance between expected success and anticipated costs when compared with *other* ways of securing its goals (and setting aside the possibility of doing nothing).

War can satisfy this second part of the assumption if either of the following statements is sometimes true:

1   War has a chance of success but there is *no* alternative to war that can also succeed; or
2   War has a chance of success as do one or more alternatives to war, but the alternatives have less chance of succeeding, will succeed in a less comprehensive way and/or will involve greater relevant costs.

Less comprehensive success would occur when, for instance, you can't save as many people from a violent threat by one alternative compared to another. By 'relevant costs', I mean infringements of basic rights, such as injury or loss of life, to innocent people. War is *necessary* in all cases of the first kind and in at least some of the second (see Lazar 2012).

As an example of the first possibility, consider how Ian Kershaw encapsulates the options open to Britain and France in the late 1930s. In contrast to the years immediately preceding the First World War, he writes, 'This time there was an obvious aggressive power whose actions increasingly closed off all options other than war – or acceptance of domination of the European continent by the tyrannical might of Nazi Germany' (Kershaw 2015: 295). As a historian, Kershaw's aim isn't to vindicate just war theory – or, for that matter, to defend the Allied war against Nazi Germany. But he directs attention towards precisely what just war theory requires in satisfaction of the conditions implied by assumption 4. By 1939, if not before, it was clearly evident that neither diplomacy nor economic pressure would dissuade Hitler from further expansion. And it was also increasingly clear that his intention was to escalate from diplomatic blackmail to simply seizing by force the territories demanded by the Reich. So war was therefore necessary in the first sense of the word: it was the only viable means of resistance.

Other examples reinforce the point that sometimes an agent is committed to executing a wrongful threat in a way that makes them impervious to any other response than force of arms. The Argentine invasion of the Falklands in 1982, for instance, pre-empted any question of diplomacy by putting soldiers on the ground and invading without prior provocation or warning. And in Rwanda in 1994, once the genocide had begun, it was unlikely to cease without swift military action by external forces – and so in the absence of any attempt to stop it, it ran its horrifying course to the end.

What these cases illustrate is something that John Locke called a 'sedate settled design' (1988 [1689]: 278). His phrase captures the mentality of someone who is determined to have their way – to take your life or your possessions or your political independence – come what may. They are not open to persuasion by appeal to reason or law and are not susceptible to non-violent coercion. The only remaining means of opposing them is force.

To illustrate the second possibility – that war might not be the only alternative but offers the best available balance of success versus cost – consider the use of economic sanctions to break the will of a regime that has aggressively seized territory. This method has been implemented against Putin's Russia, for instance, in relation to its actions in Ukraine and it was used during 1990–2003 against Saddam's regime in Iraq. Whether it is less likely to succeed than war is a contingent matter: it depends on circumstances. But it's certainly not hard to imagine war sometimes being more effective. In addition, if a regime deflects the hardship of economic sanctions onto the wider population, it can result in fatalities. And the distribution of harms might be even less discriminate than war could be, if more discriminate sanctions and suitable targets aren't available (see Cancy 2005: 249).

I can't prove assumption 4, but historical examples suggest that it is reasonable. This doesn't mean, of course, that war is always the right option in the face of threats. But sometimes it *might* be.

3.4.2 *War is always disproportionate*

Judging whether a war is *necessary* requires comparing it with all other available alternative courses of *action*. But notice that Kershaw also compared the option of war in 1939 with the possibility of doing *nothing* and accepting the Nazi domination of Europe. This comparison takes us from assessing the *necessity* of war to evaluating its *proportionality* (implicit in assumption 5).

I want to consider two possible objections to just war based on proportionality. One concerns the *jus ad bellum* more narrowly: it objects that the relevant costs of war will always exceed the relevant benefits overall. The other would argue that even if war sometimes satisfied *ad bellum* proportionality by securing a net benefit overall, the inescapable facts of contemporary armed conflict render it impossible to fight without lapsing into terrible excess. Belligerents with just cause will always be drawn into a race to the bottom, sacrificing all restraint in pursuing the ends of war. This second objection has to do with *in bello* means, which I discuss in chapter 4. For now, I'll focus on the first.

To consider this possibility, let's turn back to the case of the Second World War and the Allied fight against Nazi Germany and Imperial Japan. The Second World War as a whole took the lives of a number estimated to be in the region of 65–75 million people (Leitenberg 2006: 9).[4] Is it possible that a war that took so many lives – not to mention the destruction of spaces within which people had lived and other losses – could have been proportionate?

I think it could. The first reason is that those figures give an exaggerated impression of the costs of *deciding to fight* as distinguished from the consequences of the war taken as a whole. For although the total is extremely high, it doesn't mean that fighting had to save that many in order to be proportionate. The figure that the war would have had to save was lower owing to a number of facts.

First, many of those included in the total died fighting for the Axis powers. Their lives don't count as reasons for not fighting in the way that those of civilians killed in London during the Blitz do or even those of the Allied soldiers who died fighting against them. The soldiers of the Reich were the perpetrators of aggression and genocide. For reasons I will turn to in chapter 4, it is appropriate to give them less weight in calculating the proportionality of war.

Second, many of those who died were victims of policies that the German and Japanese regimes pursued independently of the war fought against them by the Allies. They therefore don't count *against* deciding to fight – they weighed in *favour* of war. Of course, the Allies can't claim to have saved the six million European Jews who were murdered. But neither can their deaths be placed on the 'cost' side of the ledger when evaluating the decision to resist the Nazis by force of arms.

Third, the Germans occupied some territories with hardly a shot fired. But others they seized by means of blitzkrieg. Many were killed during the invasion of Poland, for instance, as a result of German initiative and not due to a decision to defend Poland from invasion. If the military casualties were caused *independently* of a decision to resist, then they can't be counted as *costs* of resistance.

Fourth, some of the figures included belong to wars that we might say were distinct from the one (or ones) fought by the Allies against the Axis powers. The USSR, for instance, claimed many lives when seizing eastern Poland in 1939.

And finally, turning to the 'plus' side of the balance, the numbers of beneficiaries of war against the Axis powers were enormous. By 'beneficiaries', I mean those who *might have* been killed (or enslaved) if the Axis hadn't been defeated. It is their lives and basic rights that should be weighed in the balance against those that were lost or infringed as a result of fighting. In fact, unless we were able to predict exactly how long the Axis regimes would have survived had they not been resisted, the figure is entirely open-ended – there's no decisive way to put a finite upper limit on it.

To get a rough impression of the scale of what was at stake, however, we could take into account those people who would have been targets of extermination had the Nazis survived. The number of Jewish Europeans who survived the Holocaust, for instance, was roughly 3.5 million.[5] But also, anyone categorized as 'Slavic' could potentially be targeted in extermination policies, face a highly truncated life as a forced labourer or suffer forcible displacement to make room for German citizens. Take Poland, for example: in addition to the 3.5 million Polish Jews and Poles of Jewish descent who were killed there, 1.4 million 'ethnic Poles' died 'as a result of German aggression' through policies such as the extermination of national leaders and suspected or potential opponents of the Nazis. A further 2,875,500 people were deported to Germany as workers and 460,000 were displaced from territories annexed to the German state. This sort of violence was directed at a population whose pre-war total was 34.8 million (figures are from Gniazdowski 2007: 95). Anyone who had not already been murdered, uprooted and displaced, imprisoned or enslaved was exposed to a continuous threat of the same treatment as those who had gone before them.

This is to say nothing of the exposure of Asian populations (and prisoners of war) to human rights violations perpetrated by the Japanese army (see Ferguson 2006: 475–80, 496–8). Arguably, anyone exposed to the danger of German or Japanese occupation from the 1930s onwards required defence from the sorts of threat illustrated by the Polish case. They include all those who actually *were* occupied and those who were protected from occupation by the Allied war. Taking them into account alongside others from categories deemed to be inimical to the Reich or the Empire, the numbers of people defended by fighting against the Axis run into tens or even hundreds of millions.

That being the case, the discounted figure for total deaths occurring in the war as a whole – from which are subtracted the various categories indicated above – is very unlikely to exceed the number of beneficiaries. The war fought by Britain, the United States and their allies from 1939 to 1945 was proportionate, so far as casualties are concerned. And this is true even without taking into account an intractable but nevertheless vital dimension of proportionality, which is the problem of balancing costs in lives and limbs lost against gains of a more abstract kind.

I have been assuming for the sake of argument that a negative balance between rights protected and rights violated or infringed would render the war disproportionate. But it might not. The war against the Axis powers also aimed to secure values such as justice, freedom from tyranny and the protection of important rights other than rights against murder, enslavement and physical injury. There is a risk of adopting an overly reductive approach if we limit the estimate to quantifiable units of value. Walzer, for instance, forthrightly rejects the view that, 'whether we wage war against [Nazism] or not depends simply on a calculation as to the number of lives likely to be lost if there is war or peace' (Walzer 1971: 4). Similarly, the Polish government in London emphasized in 1944 that the threats faced by Poles and other occupied people 'cannot be expressed by numbers' entirely (Gniazdowski 2007: 97). There is something in the nature of certain political 'evils' that means not resisting them is not an option – the consequences of being defeated by them are 'literally beyond calculation, immeasurably awful' (Walzer 1971: 4).

3.4.3 *Warfare is always a missed opportunity*

There is, however, one other way of objecting to assumption 5. The prosecution of war generally demands that the state's political institutions and economic resources be committed to maintaining war-making capacity. If this commitment is *itself* unjustifiable, some pacifists argue, it vitiates any putative justification for each particular war (Holmes 2017: 21).

One reason why it might be unjustified is if it corrupts societies and their citizens and institutions. The danger that a concentration of military power could undermine the constitutional distribution of power is an enduring theme in political thought historically – it is prominent in Plato's *Republic*, for instance. Theorists in the modern republican tradition have at times regarded military training and discipline as necessary parts of civic virtue (e.g. Machiavelli 2003 [1521]), but there are legitimate worries from a democratic perspective about a profession that cultivates unquestioning obedience by citizens. More recently, the association of military force and gendered domination has motivated criticism from feminist theory (Hutchings 2018), as well as attempts to reconstruct just war theory in a way that takes account of gender politics (Sjoberg 2006: 9–12, and passim).

Another, perhaps more difficult, argument for the just war idea objects that military establishments divert scarce resources away from other, equally or more urgent moral demands that don't require war (Atack 2012: 170). So, for instance, it might be that missed opportunities for famine relief or disease prevention outweigh any possible gains in justice secured through war. What this argument suggests, then, is that in evaluating the option of war in a given case, we shouldn't hold the aim of defeating *this* injustice as a fixed commitment and then compare only the means of achieving *this* result for costs. We need also to consider the opportunity costs of pursuing *this* goal ahead of *other* goals that it diverts resources away from.

By way of reply, the problem that all of these arguments face is that states which forswear the use of a military force render themselves highly vulnerable to violence from less principled but better-armed states as well as non-state actors. So even if they achieved a more virtuous form of life for their citizens (and a deeper commitment to foreign aid) in the short run, in the long run they face the danger of having another form of life imposed on them by force. This is a consequence of assumption 3. Without multilateral disarmament, therefore, it seems unlikely that abolishing the armed forces in a state will achieve a lasting net improvement in satisfying higher moral standards – unless, of course, the unarmed state lives in the shadow of others that are willing to protect them, which rather begs the question.

The purpose of just war isn't entirely exhausted by each cause that it secures. It is also about maintaining security more widely for people in those states committed to morally good aims.

3.5 *Exercising judgement* ad bellum: *the case of bombing Daesh in Syria*

I have argued that the assumptions underpinning the idea of a *jus ad bellum* are reasonable and that the criteria for resorting to war can sometimes be satisfied. Satisfying them is *necessary* to justify a particular war. But I now want to suggest that it might not always be *sufficient*. Sometimes just war theory is used like an ethical pro forma. Evaluating the possibility of war involves running through the *jus ad bellum,* criterion by criterion, ticking each box in turn. If all the boxes are ticked, then war is justified (Williams 2006: 8).[6] I think justifying a resort to war is more demanding than this. It's not simply a question of taking a given possible war and asking whether it meets the criteria. First, you have to analyse the wider political context in which that possibility arose. To explore the difference this might make, let's look at the debate in December 2015 about whether Britain should participate in US bombing of Daesh targets in Syria.

Both scholars and Members of Parliament debated the point with reference to just war theory. Among the former, James Pattison argued that the bombing didn't satisfy just war criteria. Prime Minister David Cameron's case for intervention chiefly emphasized the 'defence of our citizens and our country' as the justifying cause (Cameron 2015). But the threat of violence to Europeans, Pattison suggested, was more immediately posed by Daesh sympathizers already living there than by its forces in Iraq and Syria. And the plight of the many innocent people living under Islamic State or fleeing it as refugees would only worsen, he thought, as air strikes intensified (Pattison 2015). Writing in the United States on the same issues, Michael Walzer granted that Daesh was 'an enemy that one wants to defeat,' but he too cast doubt on the prospects of success (Walzer 2015).

By contrast, Hilary Benn, a Labour MP, argued in Parliament that fighting Daesh was justified in collective defence against both a material threat to British and European citizens, and a 'fascist' ideology expressing contempt for liberal-democratic freedoms (Kettle 2015). Alan Johnson (Labour) and Mark Pritchard (Conservative), too, cited just war criteria in support of extended bombing (Hansard 2015).

The problem I want to highlight is that, while both arguments shed light on important facets of the case, neither asked an important question that should really have been asked first: which war should the United Kingdom consider fighting? In the context of the wider Syrian conflict, the answer was neither self-evident nor wholly an arbitrary matter over which there was complete discretion. It required a careful judgement of its own.

As Benn acknowledged, Britain's decision was not about declaring a new war but whether to extend the airstrikes it was *already* carrying out in Iraq across the increasingly doubtful border with Syria. This already widened the initial question: should Britain and its allies be targeting Daesh *at all* in either Iraq or Syria? But matters were even more complicated than that.

Every war, we can say, is at least three wars in one. In the simplest case, there is the war that side A wages against side B, and we can ask whether A's war is a 'just war'. Then there is the war that side B wages against side A: if A's war is unjust, then we can ask whether B's war was justified. Thirdly, we can also speak of the 'war between A and B' as a whole. But in Syria, things were even less straightforward: there was a whole alphabet of wars being fought all at once, complicating the picture still further.

Some of Syria's wars originated within the state. Others were at least partly proxy wars on behalf of foreign powers. The 'war as a whole' began in a confrontation between Assad's regime and domestic opponents. It escalated to armed conflict following Assad's decision to use military force to quell non-violent revolt, after which rebel forces emerged, some aiming to defend the opposition against violent repression (Slim 2011). So, one war, we might say, was between Assad and those carrying forward the 2011 revolt against his rule (Biggar 2013b: 396–9).

More radical elements soon took advantage of the conflict to pursue their own aims, defined by variants of al-Qaeda's Salafi Islamism (Manna 2012). Some extremists who went on to join Daesh were released by Assad from the prisons of Syria in 2011 in an attempt to make good his attempt to justify repression as counter-terrorism (Cordall 2014). The jihadist components of the opposition evolved and gained strength and it became increasingly difficult to speak of a single rebellion or a single war between the rebels and the regime.

As the conflict expanded – eventually gaining recognition as a civil 'war' by the ICRC in July 2012 – other, outside parties increased their influence. Shia Iran and Hezbollah, its proxy, offered military support to a regime that held off the prospect of another Sunni-dominated state in the region susceptible to Saudi influence. Russian forces attacked rebel targets in support of its ally, Assad, only to have its attention turned towards Daesh when a civilian aircraft was bombed by allies of the terror group in Egypt. Russia itself might be said to have been engaged in two wars, one on behalf of the regime against the rebel groups *minus* Daesh (accounting for about 70 per cent of its airstrikes by February 2016) (Wintour, Chulov and Black 2016); the other, for its own reasons, against Daesh in particular.

By December 2015, Daesh was party to a cluster

of wars. On the one hand, it was part of the wider Sunni rebellion against Assad. On the other, it aimed to dismantle both Syria and Iraq, replacing them with a new 'Islamic State'. It also waged war against ethnic and religious minorities – notably the Kurdish and Yazidi peoples – and then turned its attention to fighting a terrorist war against European and other western states.

From the perspective of the 'greater war' that began in 2011 and that then saw so many 'lesser wars' break out as its constantly mutating parts, it hardly seems sufficient to apply just war criteria without further ado to Britain's decision about whether to extend its venture from Iraq to Syria. We need first to ask how that war would fit within the wider complex of Syrian wars and the competing descriptions of what was going on in it.

The United Kingdom's plan looked most likely to satisfy just war conditions if it was described as part of a war against Daesh fought by Britain and its allies. More than simply a 'terrorist' group in any familiar sense (Byman 2015), its methods both in the region and abroad involved grotesque public displays of violence against innocent people (civilians, members of religious minorities or rival ethnicities, gay people and others who exercised what would be regarded by democracies as liberal freedoms). The rhetorical force of Benn's characterization of the group as 'fascist' stemmed from the fact that it seemed determined to realize something like a totalitarian form of rule built on profound intolerance (Gray 2014). And, even if its agents abroad were often local recruits in Europe and the United States, the impetus for their missions often issued from Daesh itself.

So if we narrowed our focus to evaluating the decision of December 2015 as part of a war by Britain and its allies against Daesh, then there was at least a strong prima facie case that it had just cause. But there is a problem with accepting that description. Both Daesh *and* Assad (not to mention Russia) had a strategic interest in redefining and narrating the Syrian war in the same way. Assad had long sought to frame the conflict as a war on 'terror', thereby elbowing himself into the international coalition that the United States sought to forge after 9/11. Likewise, Daesh had its own favourite narrative which defined the conflict as a war of true Islam against polytheism, atheism and apostasy. Guided by this description, Daesh sought to goad states like the United Kingdom into a fight that it calculated would stoke resentment amongst Sunni Muslims in the region and elsewhere (Wood 2015).

To regard the United Kingdom's involvement in Syria as a 'just war,' therefore, relies on a description of the conflict in terms that both Assad and then Daesh had worked hard to engineer, which must surely raise concerns. There was an alternative. This was to resist the Assad–Daesh narratives by viewing the conflict from perspectives they sought to obscure from view: above all, those of the majority of people in Syria who desperately needed to see an end to both of these violently oppressive rivals. To do so required defining the war through the eyes of those who first stood up to the regime and those rebels who even by 2015 aimed at something better than replacing one violent dictatorship with another (Walzer 2013). From their point of view, the conflict was a war between the Assad regime and the people that it was its responsibility to protect but whom it continued to slaughter as a means of clinging onto power (OHCHR 2016).

The problem for the United Kingdom was that, from the perspective of rebellion against Assad, the bombing of Daesh was a mixed blessing. On the one hand, Daesh was a dangerous rival that those pursuing a true improvement on the Assad regime regarded as an enemy. But on the other, by waging war *only* against Daesh, the United States, France and Britain became de facto military allies of

Assad and Russia. Without twinning it with a viable strategy for replacing Assad's government with something better, the war against Daesh attempted to defeat a lesser evil at the expense of bolstering what had so far proven to be a significantly greater one (Syrian Network for Human Rights 2015).

This is a further reason to follow Pattison, Walzer and others in questioning the justice of war against Daesh in Syria. Whether there was an all-things-considered justification for the decision that the Westminster MPs supported in December 2015 is something I will leave readers to judge. But the example shows how treating the *jus ad bellum* as a simple checklist could give rise to morally and politically questionable results – it could potentially legitimate unjust wars or fail to permit just ones (cf. Finlay 2017b). An appropriate use of the just war criteria, by contrast, ought to occur as part of a wider, richer, more nuanced political analysis.

4

Fighting Just Wars: Balancing Ends and Means

But our problems are not quite over. What if war necessarily requires people to do things that are sufficiently evil in themselves to vitiate any good that fighting them might achieve? So even if wars were sometimes necessary in the sense explored in section 3.4.1 and proportionate in their objective results (rights defended versus lives and limbs lost, for instance), fighting them is still morally worse than letting evil run its course because of the methods they involve. If so, then there would still be a problem with assumption 5.

I'll address the different parts of this problem in three waves: section 4.1 considers age-old problems that just war theory has absorbed through its classic doctrines; section 4.2 considers the objection that organized killing and status-based targeting are inherently objectionable; and section 4.3 considers the worry that wars with just cause might require violations of *jus in bello* alongside other moral compromises *post bellum*.

4.1 Doing, allowing and intending harm

4.1.1 Deliberate and collateral killing

Theorists have had to find ways to address two related problems concerning the means of fighting just wars. The first arises from the Doctrine of Doing and Allowing, according to which there seems to be a moral asymmetry between doing harm to someone and merely allowing it to befall them: causing harm in the first way is often harder to justify than being linked to it in the latter way. I won't argue one way or the other as to the validity of the doctrine on its traditional formulations, which are contested (see, for instance, Draper 2015: ch. 3). But I will assume for the sake of argument that the general idea is right. If so, it suggests a problem for my interpretation of just war theory: if *doing* harm to individuals is harder to justify than *allowing* others to suffer harm, then it suggests we need to clarify why we might believe assumption 5 to be true.

The second problem is this: serious attempts to prosecute war in modern conditions require weapons that often harm not only their intended targets but also civilian bystanders. 'Collateral damage' seems unavoidable. It is pointless to insist that just warriors forswear the use of such weapons because, even if they did, it's unlikely that their enemies would do so. And if these weapons bestow significant military advantages, then just wars pose a difficult choice: use them and you might win, but at the cost of harming innocent bystanders; refuse them, and you respect their immunity but lose the war.

Without some further intellectual equipment, then, the core convictions of just war theory are pitted against each other. We could (a) insist on observing strict moral restraint (following from conviction III), but then we no longer seem to be able to justify war in exceptional cases (conviction II). So only convictions I and III remain standing and just war proves impossible. Or, if we thought the goals of just war important enough, perhaps (b) we might accept that wrongful methods could still be adopted, leaving the possibility of an exceptional justification for war standing (conviction II). But the cost would be abandoning the third defining conviction (III): that war must be fought with moral restraint.

For all three convictions to be upheld, we need to find a route through the gulf between contingent pacifism that results from (a) and the *in bello* realism arising from (b) (see Walzer 1977: ch. 1).

4.1.2 Liability to attack

As regards doing harm and allowing it, the first reply is very simple: doing harm is worse than allowing it *all else being equal*. Where all else is *not* equal, then the doctrine doesn't always prohibit harming. Doing harm to a smaller number of people might be less morally bad than allowing harm to a much larger number of people.

This takes us one step towards a solution to the difficulty, but it still leaves us some way short. What if the people you were harming were innocent? They are not the source of wrongful threat or responsible for it. If so, then the difference between harms caused and harms averted would have to be very great indeed before you could justify violence (Coady 2008: ch. 8; Finlay 2015: ch. 9; Walzer 1977: ch. 16). Unless there are other factors, narrowing this gap in some way, 'just war' would be very hard to justify.

This is where the theory of 'liability' to harm comes into play. Recent debate on this idea has been intense and there is ongoing controversy about how to interpret it. But the main thought is this: if someone is responsible for a wrongful threat; and if the only (or sometimes even the best) way to diminish that threat is to harm them; then harming doesn't *wrong* them. At least, it doesn't wrong them so long as the harm they suffer isn't disproportionate to the threat it prevents and to the degree to which the target is responsible for the threat.[1]

The classic sort of case that illustrates this possibility sees someone is attacked without provocation. Consider the following hypothetical:

Murderer: A habitual murderer wishes to kill someone. You happen to be the first person he encounters on the day he plans to commit his next random killing. He finds you alone in a deserted street and approaches you, declaring his intention and raising a knife. But you possess a pistol (let's say legally). The only way to save your life is to shoot him, which will probably result in his death.

What are you permitted to do in this scenario?

Those who are not absolute, 'personal' pacifists (e.g. Tolstoy 1974 [1893]: 372–3) would say that defensive killing is justifiable here. Most people, I presume, would *also* agree that the right of self-defence isn't symmetrical: it can't be claimed back against you by the murderer. You have the right because you are innocent and the attacker has compelled you to choose between allowing him to kill you and resorting to force. He has no right of self-defence because he is responsible for your predicament. He has the right to surrender and, if he did so and gave you sufficient assurances of his sincerity, then you would probably be obliged not to kill him (and to call the police for assistance instead). But unless he has done so, his interest in continuing to live doesn't carry its normal weight in deciding what to do. And, lastly, I imagine most people would agree that if a third party was able to defend the victim but only by killing the murderer, then they would have a prima facie justification for doing so.

If the murderer is *liable* to be killed, then it suggests that *doing* harm in similar cases is not worse than *allowing* it. Turning, then, to the possibility of war with a just cause, if those to whom it is necessary to *do* harm are generally liable to be harmed, then it means that assumption 5 is more likely (all else being equal) to be true. Liability is the reason why the lives of combatants contributing to wrongful threats have diminished weight in assessing whether war is proportionate, *ad bellum*, as I suggested in section 3.4.2.

4.1.3 *The Doctrine of Double Effect*

So, if the prosecution of war only harmed people who were liable to attack, then justification wouldn't be impossible. But modern war always harms the innocent. Many suffer as a *foreseeable* but *unintended* result of otherwise legitimate attacks. This is widely cited as a key objection against targeted killings using drones, and it is an even bigger worry in assessing the use of weapons such as aerial bombardment and artillery. Can this objection be addressed?

The answer is sourced by just war theory in an idea attributed to Thomas Aquinas: the Doctrine of Double Effect (DDE) (Aquinas in Reichberg, Syse and Begby 2006: 190–1; McIntyre 2014; Walzer 1977: 151–9). The DDE reflects the idea that one action can have multiple effects. Some are intended, others not. Sometimes, it may be permissible to cause harm as a foreseeable but unintended consequence of one's action that it wouldn't have been permissible to cause intentionally (FitzPatrick 2012: 183). Just war theorists cite the doctrine to zone in on harmful consequences affecting innocent people that are foreseeable but truly unavoidable. Sometimes the only way to attack a legitimate target will necessarily risk inflicting side-effect harms on civilians. If so, then in deciding whether to carry it out, we have to ask whether (a) there is genuinely no other way to achieve an equivalent military goal with lower risks, and (b) whether the target is valuable enough, militarily (and, hence, when fighting for a just cause, morally) to justify the likely civilian casualties. If the answer to both questions is yes, then it is thought the action is permissible.

The upshot of this idea is that an action that harms non-combatants foreseeably but unintentionally is more likely to be justified than one that requires harming the same number deliberately. In the case of deliberate targeting, the inherent wrongfulness of intentionally causing harms to innocent people also has to be weighed against the duty to defend those on whose behalf the action is taken. And wrongs of this sort *almost always* mean that acting is morally worse than not acting. But in cases where the harms to the innocent are genuinely the unavoidable side effects of an otherwise permissible action, then whether it is justified comes down to a more direct comparison of consequences: lives saved by acting may be weighed against lives lost by acting.

The significance of the DDE has been questioned by philosophers who doubt that the permissibility of actions is really about intentions rather than about objective reasons. But, even so, there is little disagreement about the belief that it has generally been thought to explain: that it may be justifiable to commit acts causing harms that are not part of their aim, provided those harms aren't out of proportion to the values sought by means of those acts. If we can accept this conclusion, then the inevitability of collateral damage won't always stand in the way of just war.

4.2 *Justified violence; justified war?*

What I want to argue is that if (a) we think individuals have basic human rights against wrongful lethal violence and similar threats, and (b) we agree that they have the right to be defended against these threats in some circumstances, then we should accept (c) that there will be a *jus ad bellum* in some imaginable cases. This may take different forms including defensive war against international aggression, intervention on behalf of the victims of human rights violations, armed resistance and revolutionary war within oppressive states, and defensive force against terrorist organizations.

Let's call this set of possible just wars 'defensive war'. There is a further, deeper problem with this category which we now need to examine. Whereas individual self-defence might be justifiable, some pacifists concede, war nevertheless is not. The reason for this is repugnance at the idea of the 'deliberate, organized and systematic use of force to harm or kill persons' (Holmes 2017: 16) and at the institutions that support it. Let's call this practice 'warfare'. I will tease out the objection – or one interpretation of it – before I attempt a reply.

4.2.1 *Defensive war; offensive attack*
One way to specify the problem with warfare is to start with the individual's right against being killed and her right to be defended. Trying to apply individual defensive rights directly to the sort of extensive, coordinated violence typical of warfare seems, at first glance, to raise some problems of consistency.

Imagine it's late in the Second World War and you are a soldier in the British army, advancing against the retreating *Wehrmacht*. Are you permitted to try to kill German soldiers only if they are presently engaged in attacks imminently threatening someone? Not according to conventional wisdom, and in this respect I think it is correct: as long as they aren't surrendering, you may attack enemy soldiers at any time, whether they are attacking, retreating or standing still. Even if your war is rightfully described (and justified) as a *defensive* one taken as a whole, you are permitted actions as an individual contributor to that war that are tactically or strategically *offensive*. In this respect, *just war* differs sharply from *individual rights of self-defence*, at least in the form they take in other contexts. On the face of it, offensive tactics seem to involve targeting individuals based on their membership of a category ('enemy soldiers'), rather than on anything attributable to individual moral agency. Can this really be consistent with individual rights (to life and to its defence)?

For the purposes of the argument set out in chapter 2, failing to explain offensive killing would be deeply troubling for the just war theorist. The assumptions set out in section 2.2 support core conviction II only if *warfare* in particular, and not just individual defensive killing, is less vicious than the evils it may be used to defeat. It will therefore be necessary to show how this sort of status-based killing can be reconciled with the rights of the individual.

4.2.2 *The right to life and to self-defence*
For someone living in a law-governed state in peacetime, defensive rights generally occur only against *imminent* attack.[2] This is because violent

defence is usually necessary only when faced with someone already engaging in an assault or patently about to do so.[3] Trying to apply this model of defensive rights directly to defensive war faces three problems: *uncertainty*, *over-determination* and *under-determination*. These factors make it harder to see how the sorts of killing likely to be required by a just war are individually necessary to defend individuals.

To clarify what I mean by *uncertainty*, compare the offensive wartime killing described above to the scenario set out by the recent movie *Eye in the Sky* (2015) in which UK decision makers can literally see the belts being fitted onto the suicide bombers prior to a planned attack. Where the threat is as certain as this, we can say that defensive killing is necessary in quite a strict sense. By contrast, killing in war often involves attacking people who are not imminently going to attack anyone. You can guess by their uniform and perhaps location that they *might* kill or harm people at some point. But you are permitted to attack them even if they pose no immediate threat and might not go on to do so.

One way to account for the permission to kill them in such a case would be to loosen the restriction implied by the necessity and imminence conditions, permitting attacks against those who pose a *risk* of future attack. But this would give too much discretion to decision makers considering the use of defensive force outside of a wartime context.[4] In effect, the implication would be to redefine the underlying normative basis for justified defence from the right *not to be killed wrongfully* to a right *not to face any risk of being killed wrongfully*. Whereas the former permits lethal defensive force only against those violating basic rights, the latter could license attacks on people who had not (yet) done anything wrong: they might only be committed to a hostile ideology or be associated closely enough with the wrong people in order to be considered a credible risk. If we think that killing people with similarly tenuous connections to threats to be unjustifiable in peacetime but justifiable in war, then we need a way to draw a distinction between peace and war that explains the difference.

The problems of *under-* and *over-determination* occur when the target is, as it were, just a cog in the machine. *Under-determination* occurs when someone occupies a non-pivotal role in a group committed to wrongfully threatening others. Killing them might have some slight effect on future attacks, perhaps by making the remaining participants work harder to launch them. But doing so cannot be described as necessary to *eliminate* (or even significantly diminish) the threat. *Over-determination* arises when a wider organization poses the threat and the individual enemy is just a foot soldier, so to speak. If *she* doesn't carry out an order to kill, then someone else will take her place. Again, if this is the case, then we cannot really say that killing her is necessary to save lives because killing her alone won't have that effect. As long as there are substitutes, then the enemy force will simply replace her when the time comes for attack.

I presume that a successful defensive war will target many individuals who are not engaged in an imminent attack against identifiable victims. Consequently, if we tried to interpret and evaluate each killing on its own terms as part of an iterative series of defensive actions, many wouldn't satisfy the requirement of necessity due to one or more of these three problems. If such attacks are justifiable, then it must be on a different footing.

4.2.3 *Collective threats; collective defence*
The tension between defensive ethics and the offensive nature of warfare occupied the minds of just war theorists in earlier centuries. Their solution was to argue that just war must be interpreted as an extension of the state's right to punish wrongdoers (Grotius 2012 [1625]: 89; Vitoria 1991 [1539]:

300). Just war theorists nowadays find this interpretation unattractive (Luban 2011). To find a better explanation, we need to work step by step from the rights with which we started out.

Let's start with *uncertainty*. Even in cases where we're unsure whether killing *this* target is necessary to diminish a particular threat, we might yet know that she belongs to an organization that threatens harm. And even if we didn't know which particular targets were at risk, we could still be 100 per cent certain that the organization is going to attack somewhere. So we could be confident that degrading the capacity of the organization to which Enemy Soldier$_1$ belongs is necessary to eliminate a threat. And attacking enemy soldiers is likely to be part of the means of doing so.

Once we know that there is an organized threat, then it may be possible to address the problems of *under-* and *over-determination*, too. Killing Enemy Soldier$_1$ might be unlikely to diminish their organization's overall capacity significantly when considered as a one-off act. It is therefore hard to see it as necessary considered in isolation. But a series of such attacks could diminish the organization's collective capacity cumulatively. You could therefore describe killing Enemy Soldier$_1$ as a necessary part of defending against the threat, provided you knew that Enemy Soldier$_2$, Enemy Soldier$_3$ and so on were also going to be eliminated.

Likewise, if Enemy Soldier$_1$ was simply first in the queue for the next attack by the enemy organization and, if eliminated, would be replaced by Enemy Soldier$_2$, then killing him *alone* might do nothing to prevent a possible future attack. But if we knew that it would be followed up by a series of similar strikes, each taking out a successive member of the enemy's fighting forces, then we might be able to justify it. Doing so as an isolated, single action would not achieve the necessary result. But, as part of an ongoing, collectively organized series of such actions, it might.

So whereas some violent acts may be justified purely on their own terms (those that resemble *Eye in the Sky*, for instance), others seem to be justifiable only if they occur against a more complex background. First, there would have to be a collectively organized threat. This would explain how targeting an individual not presently posing a personal threat could serve defensive purposes. Second, a soldier engaging in such an attack would need to know that they were doing so as part of a coordinated defensive response to that threat. For this to be credible, she would need to know, thirdly, that there was an authoritative *strategy*. It would be authoritative both in the sense that there are grounds to believe that it satisfies the conditions of success, necessity and proportionality, and in the sense that enough soldiers are willing to follow it. And finally, there needs to be some form of leadership competent to identify the collective threat, formulate the strategy and coordinate individuals to implement it.

In cases where these conditions are present, the problem identified in 4.2.1 can be solved. Instead of trying to justify war by showing how it may be built up out of a cluster of individually justified defensive acts, we need to work things out in reverse order. The justification for individual acts of killing in war depends on a prior justification for collectively coordinated warfare.

4.3 *Conflicts between* jus ad bellum *and the conduct of war and peace*

So far, I have concentrated on intended harms to combatants and unintended harm to people not liable to attack. Both are compatible with *jus in bello* as it is generally understood in just war theory. But what if defensive wars sometimes require their protagonists to violate the *jus in bello* and other just war principles in order to succeed? The problem in a nutshell is this: *if* just war requires strict adherence to the *jus in bello* and all other just war conditions; and *if* wars fought for a just cause generally require violations of these conditions in order to succeed, *then* just war is (generally) impossible. A defence of the possibility of just war needs to address this.

4.3.1 *Falling short of the just war ideal: the case of the Second World War*

The most dramatic way in which wars fought for a just cause fall short of the just war ideal is by violating the moral principles of the *jus in bello*. Larry May, for instance, writes that:

> Many believe that there have been just causes to go to war, such as to stop Nazi aggression and genocide in the Second World War. But if one considers such World War II tactics as fire-bombing and carpet bombing, as well as dropping the atomic bomb on a population centre, even the Second World War was not clearly a just war. (May 2015: 3)

If just war is defined by the moral purity of the means employed in its execution, then May is right. This would be a problem for my argument because, like many others, I believe this is the most promising example we have and, without it, it is much harder to imagine defending the possibility of just war successfully.

But, in fact, the problem is even worse. At least two additional features stand out starkly when we judge the execution of war against Germany by the standards of just war theory. One is the alliance between democratic opponents of Hitler and the Soviet Union. Both Britain and France were imperial powers that had used repressive measures in their colonies, which already raises questions about their legitimacy as agents of just war. But the inclusion of the USSR as an ally deepens the problem further. The other problem concerns standards of justice *post bellum*. Reliance on the Red Army during the war also resulted in a compromise with Stalin, leading to the post-war Soviet occupation of Eastern Europe, the partition of Germany and the establishment of puppet communist regimes. There were other compromises too. The failure to prosecute large numbers of Nazis was due in part by a perceived need to shore up West Germany as a bulwark *against* the USSR and the eastern-European communist regimes (see Fabre 2016: ch. 7; Judt 2010: ch. 2).

For all three of these moral compromises, there are two possibilities. Either the compromise *was* in fact necessary to the Allied war – without it, the war would have been lost. Or it wasn't necessary (for a sceptical view on the effectiveness of allied bombing, for instance, see Overy 2013). Either way, we have an important question to think about. On the first assumption, we have to consider the possibility that the most important example of ostensibly just war that we have necessarily involved means that fall foul of core principles of *jus in bello* and postwar justice. If this means that the Second World War was *not* a just war, then it lends support to the view that just war is *not possible*. But, on the second assumption, there's another problem: war, it might be argued, is never executed correctly according to the standards of justice, even when one might do so without losing. Human nature, error, ignorance, weakness and fear ensure that just war in the full sense of the term – war that satisfies all appropriate moral standards – is, in a very practical sense, impossible.

So where should we stand on the idea of the Second World War as a 'just war' between the Allies and Germany? Do any of these facets of the historical case prove that it was *not* a just war? Or can the case of war against Nazism still be cited in support of the claim that just war is, in fact, possible?

4.3.2 *The just war paradigm*

My view is that the Allied fight against the Nazis in the Second World War (to say nothing of the war against Japan) *was* a just war. I have two arguments for this.

One is based on the interpretation I have offered of just war's underlying assumptions. Recall the fifth assumption: '(5) that sometimes the wrong of failing to impede or prevent the injustices threatened by others would be greater than the (prima facie) wrong of those killings that impeding or preventing them would require.' The demand that war be less evil in this sense than the evil it defeats doesn't necessarily require satisfying the principles of *jus in bello* and *jus post bellum* entirely. Even without resorting to a purely consequentialist analysis, war might fall short of these standards and yet still satisfy the demand implicit in assumption 5. We might agree, for instance, that non-combatant immunity is a 'deadly serious convention', as Jeremy Waldron has argued (2010). But defeating an evil like Nazism should surely also be seen as a 'deadly serious cause' (Finlay 2018). Both convention and cause refer to extremely weighty duties. If they run into conflict, then it will be necessary to compromise on one for the sake of the other. Sometimes this may mean giving up on a fight for the sake of restraint (i.e. prioritizing conviction III over II). But it is also likely that sometimes a war might deviate from the *jus in bello* and yet involve fewer (prima facie) wrongs than non-resistance (or failure to win) overall.[5] Whether it does is another difficult matter of moral and political judgement.

The other argument has to do with the special status of the war against Nazism as a *paradigm* in twentieth-century just war theory. In *The Structure of Scientific Revolutions* (1996 [1962]), Thomas Kuhn argued that fundamental shifts in the methods and theoretical programme of science could be accounted for with reference to certain exemplary ('paradigmatic') practices. These were cases where, for instance, a particular scientist demonstrated the potential for doing things in a new way with a singularly successful piece of research. If the example was sufficiently at odds with established practice, and if it captured the imagination of enough scientists and with sufficient force, then it could lead to a 'paradigm shift': a move from modelling scientific practice on an older example to one modelled on the new example.

I think the fight against Nazism in the Second World War has paradigmatic status in twentieth-century just war theory. The theory was reshaped and its standing renewed after 1945 by the example of a war against extraordinary evil. Such was its nature that it became much harder to conceive of an argument that supported the idea of non-resistance in at least such extreme cases. An evil of this magnitude had to be resisted, *even if* it required resorting to extreme tactical measures and political compromise.

If the war against the Nazis is paradigmatic in this sense, then it means that our judgements about the credibility of morally justified warfare are based on the example and not the other way round. And because the paradigm involved significant deviations from *jus in bello* and *jus post bellum,* they have come to be possibilities that post-war just war theory has had to find ways to absorb (e.g. Walzer on 'Supreme Emergency' in 1977: ch. 16 and 2004: 33–50).

4.3.3 *Reflective equilibrium*

On the other hand, the value of just war theory resides in its utility as a framework for judging cases as well as for guiding action.[6] And even if its credibility now relies to some extent on prior judgements about fighting the Nazis, there must surely be some way of using it to evaluate the details of the Second World War, alongside other examples. To account for this, I think we have to work back and forth between what a theory might *ideally* stipulate and our judgements concerning the paradigm case until we find the right balance.

So, on the one hand, if the Second World War is *paradigmatic*, then the plausibility of debating just war theory and applying it to *other* cases is supported by a belief that fighting the Nazis was justified. If so, then the theory cannot defeat the case without undermining itself. It is therefore necessary, when working out what the best theory would look like, to do so with an eye on the Second World War and to treat the theory as in some way an attempt to make sense of our considered judgements about that war. But it is also necessary to take the argument back in the opposite direction and judge particular facets of the case in light of the best theory. If we can frame just war theory and our judgement about the Second World War in a way that permits us both to validate the public judgement that fighting the Nazis was justified *and* still be able to criticize the Allies' conduct of the Second World War in light of the theory, then we will have achieved what Rawls calls 'reflective equilibrium' (1971): this is a harmonious balance between our considered judgements about particular cases and the principles we will use to judge further cases. In order to achieve this balance, I believe we have to adopt a particular version of what might be called a 'non-ideal' theory of justified war (cf. Pattison 2018).

5

Conclusion:
Just Wars, Ideal and
Non-Ideal

So, the Allied war against the Nazis didn't meet the
standards of just war theory across its three major
dimensions, *ad bellum, in bello* or *post bellum*.
The motives and aims even of the protagonists
were probably tainted; the methods they used were
certainly unsound in many instances; and the post-
war order they negotiated bore the stamp of the de
facto balance of power in 1945, rather than that of
justice in any pure sense.[1] But in a way, of *course*
this was true. No human endeavour – collective,
coordinated and complex – is ever perfect. But this
doesn't necessarily mean that all such endeavours
are unjustified. The real question in each case is
this: is it justifiable to initiate and engage with this
endeavour, compromised as it undoubtedly will be
in the execution?

To answer that question in any given case, I

think we need to answer another, prior one: is just war in a *pure* sense possible – in principle – at the point of initiating it? So, for instance, was a just war possible in the circumstances of September 1939, when Britain and France declared war on Germany? Sure, we might say, we won't fight *that* war precisely: some people will fail to exercise judgement adequately; others will choose to do the wrong thing while fighting. There will be mistakes and there will be crimes. But if everyone on our side committed themselves to discharging their responsibilities and to exercising judgement to the highest possible degree in fighting this way, would it be a just war in all respects? If the answer is 'no', then we need to ask: would it be an all-things-considered justifiable war? So even if, say, it was necessary to deviate from the laws of war so far as the methods of fighting were concerned in order to win it, would those deviations be limited enough to escape vitiating the good of winning?

According to the idea of the just war as I have presented it in this book, only if the answer to both these questions is 'no', is there categorically no possible justification for fighting. But if it is 'yes' (to either, not just the first question), then there might be, and it becomes a matter of careful judgement. Whether, in fact, there is a justification for fighting a war now *in practice* depends on the degree to which participants in the otherwise just war are likely to fail to comply with what it requires and how far the actual war as fought will fall short of the 'just war' as it ought to have been conducted.

The bottom line, I believe, is indicated by assumption 5. One suggestion for capturing the sort of judgement it requires that might seem plausible is, as May puts it, that the war as fought would 'have to cause fewer violations of rights than protection of rights' (2015: 3). But this would only capture part of the picture that we need to judge. What assumption 5 entails, I think, is a richer conception of what we could call 'moral' proportionality. As a criterion of *jus ad bellum*, proportionality requires a net positive balance in the relevant results of war. But a positive result measured purely in rights protected might be achieved in a variety of different ways. A discriminate war might achieve it, for instance, in which case all is well. But what if the only means of achieving it were to fight a wholly indiscriminate war? Then war might be unjustified *ad bellum* in spite of apparently satisfying proportionality. This is because the wrongfulness of the means is likely to outweigh the viciousness of failing to prevent the evils against which the war is to be fought. In which case, the war proposed fails by a richer, moral criterion of proportionality, one implied by assumption 5: the killing and violence required by fighting the war must not be morally worse than the prima facie wrong of not defending those under threat.

If my argument is correct, then judgements about whether war is *morally* proportionate are finely balanced. In light of the Second World War as a paradigm, they can't be pre-packaged as an injunction against any and all wars that violate the 'deadly serious conventions' enshrined in the LOAC. Instead, they have to compare the viciousness of the means with the viciousness of failing to secure the ends in each case and decide which way the balance tilts. On this account, the most serious causes might demand some degree of derogation from the standard *jus in bello* where doing so is necessary.

So wars that conform to assumption 5 are *justified*. Even if they don't wholly satisfy the 'ideal' conditions of the just war, either according to some purely theoretical ideal[2] or according to the best war possible in the circumstances, it is still justifiable to initiate them and participate in them. And surely there is a strong sense in which 'just war' *means* 'justified war' (see Fabre on 'justified' peace in 2016: 17–20; cf. McMahan 2005: 15–16)? To think otherwise seems to me to involve a category mistake: it implies that 'war' can realize a conception of justice in the same way as a person of good character might do in the course of a well-lived life or a good society in the composition of its core institutions. 'Just war' cannot, surely, mean 'war that realizes the ideals of justice' per se: war by its very nature is something that presupposes a failure to realize those ideals. When we say 'just war', we mean that the war in question contributes to a better chance of realizing a society whose institutions express a reasonable conception of justice or that it protects and helps to secure one of them (on the first possibility, see Finlay 2015: ch. 2).

On my interpretation, just war is *not* exclusively or even first and foremost about restraint. Rather, it is about three objectives that are often in tension with one another: first, to *permit* war in those cases where it is justified; second, to prohibit war in all other cases; and, third, to insist on maximum possible restraint in its execution. Just war theory, then, is centrally about striking the right balance. If we interpret just war theory in light of the five underlying assumptions identified in chapter 2, it permits us to work out the balance in a fairly flexible way that is responsive to what circumstances demand. On this approach, we will view the question of restraint in light of the need to fight successfully in circumstances of dire necessity – which are the only circumstances in which the resort to war should be contemplated. The theory I offer probably makes more room, therefore, for the demands of necessity than some traditional accounts.

Let me close with the question of how likely it is that just wars will occur in the current world order. Since 1945, international war has become a significantly less pronounced feature of international politics than it was during the previous century or so. There are several reasons that might help account for this. One is that US hegemony provided the world with a 'global policeman' – particularly after the decline of the USSR – that was able to prevent it. Nuclear deterrence, secondly, might have done something to disincentivize open armed conflict between states. The spread of democracy has been seen by various scholars as an important factor in reducing the propensity to international aggression (on the assumption that democracies are less prone to instigate war, at least between themselves). Globalization has also altered the balance of pros and cons when comparing war to alternatives on the parts of states whose interests are increasingly intertwined (Gat 2017). And, finally, the development of international law, as one recent study particularly argues, has had an important effect through the prohibition on using war as an instrument of state policy since the Kellogg–Briand Pact outlawed it in 1928 (Hathaway and Shapiro 2017).

If aggressive wars are less common, then it would seem likely that just cause for war will be less frequent too. But there are a number of reasons to doubt this. First, wars involving non-state parties have become increasingly prevalent during the same era. This raises two possibilities: first, that just wars might occur when legitimate governments have to try to defeat threats in the form of terrorist insurgencies; and second, that they may occur when illegitimate governments are the target for non-state rebel or revolutionary forces compelled to pursue liberation and justice by military means.

Second, if 'America led the world in constructing an architecture to keep the peace . . .' (Obama 2009), the apparent decline in US power already seems to have contributed to a reduction in global stability.[3] The annexation of Crimea and wider interference in Ukraine (and elsewhere) by Russia may betoken the start of an era in which the seizure of foreign territory occurs more often than it did in recent decades (and it had never entirely disappeared, as the expansion of Israel into the West Bank and East Jerusalem in 1967 and Iraq's invasion of Kuwait in 1990 illustrate). If insurgent states – as well as non-state groups like al-Qaeda and Daesh – become more active, then the chances of war becoming necessary in one context or another become greater. Paradoxically, then, the decline in stability of the current world order is likely to create *more* incidence of unjust threat and, consequently, a greater likelihood of just war rather than less. The problems that just war theory equips us to address are therefore unlikely to disappear. As long as exigencies of this kind remain possible, there remains the possibility of a just war and therefore just war theory retains its importance as a critical part of political theory.

Notes

Preface

1 For criticism of just war theory based on its relationship with colonialism, see for instance Kochi (2009,
2013). See also Zurbuchen (2009).

Chapter 1 Ideas and Ideals of the Just War

1 Though, as Pablo Kalmanovitz (2018) argues, this
ideal demands that warring parties act in good faith
according to a publicly defended belief that they
were engaged in substantively just war, i.e. that they
possessed a case according to the principles of *jus ad
bellum*.
2 Compare accounts of the equality or inequality of
just versus unjust warriors in Fabre (2012), Frowe
(2014), Lazar (2015), McMahan (2009) and Walzer
(1977), and the views collected in Rodin and Shue
(2008). For a review of current debate, see Lazar
(2017a, 2017b).

3 For attempts to offer alternative accounts showing how war could be justified where 'lesser' values
than life and limb as such are at stake, see Fabre
(2012); Finlay (2015); Iser (2017: 207–26); and Frowe
(2014).

Chapter 3 'Just Cause' and the Possibility of Jus ad Bellum

1 Hume thought that the rulers of states owed a limited
set of weaker, negative duties towards one another,
chiefly to do with respecting property.
2 Hume himself believed that even in the international
realm, some thinner forms of moral convention had
arisen between princes, and he appreciated the benefits arising from growing commerce between nations
during the eighteenth century.
3 For challenges to Schmitt's reading of early modern
natural law theory, see Kalmanovitz (2018) and
Teschke (2016).
4 Cf. Burleigh (2010: ix) who gives 55 million as the
figure and Walzer (1971: 4) who worked from an
estimate of 30,000,000 in his analysis of the Second
World War.
5 See DellaPergola (1993: 34). This is a rough estimate
based on the total Jewish population in Europe in
1939, which DellaPergola estimates at 9.5 million,
and subtracting the number generally thought to have
died in the Holocaust.
6 See Bellamy (2006: ch. 6) for discussion of some other
theoretical issues that complicate the picture further

and Buchanan (2018) for an argument for a 'richer' *jus ad bellum*.

Chapter 4 Fighting Just Wars: Balancing Ends and Means

1 For the contrast between 'comparative' and 'non-comparative' views on responsibility and liability, see the review in Lazar (2015: 4–5). For a classic account of war ethics based on individual moral responsibility and liability, see McMahan (2009).

2 On imminence, see Waldron (2010: 107) and the Joint Committee (2016: 8). For an account of defensive rights that takes imminence to be an 'intrinsic limitation,' see Rodin (2002).

3 According to Article 2 of the European Convention on Human Rights, for instance, killing someone doesn't violate their right to life as long as it arises from a 'use of force which is no more than absolutely necessary [to defend] any person from unlawful violence' (2.2.a).

4 For an attempt to redefine 'imminence' in order to encompass these sorts of case in the context of targeted operations against terrorism suspects, see the US Department of Justice White Paper on the lawfulness of 'a lethal operation' against US citizens in a senior position in al-Qaeda (Department of Justice 2011: 8).

5 On the different types and degrees of deviation from the 'standard *jus in bello*' that might be possible, see Finlay (2015: chs 4, 8 and 9).

6 On the complexities of the relationship between just war theory and political action, see Buchanan (2018).

Chapter 5 Conclusion:
Just Wars, Ideal and Non-Ideal

1 Fiala (2008) sees the just war idea as a myth due to the fact that its ideal conditions are so seldom satisfied.
2 The one in which everyone on the just side does their very best to discharge all duties.
3 On the decline of US power and the erosion of global moral norms, see Tooze (2016); see also Tooze (2015). David Luban (2004: 210) argues that just war theory functions as a 'general doctrine' in a Westphalian system of 'equal sovereign states' but considers doubts about its suitability as such in an era of US military pre-eminence. My point is that US hegemony has also been an important factor in establishing just war principles as general doctrines for world order. On the important question of how just war doctrines relate to an institutional background internationally, see Buchanan (2006, 2018).

References

Abdul-Ahad, Ghaith (2017) 'After the Liberation of Mosul an Orgy of Killing', *The Guardian*, 21 November, https://www.theguardian.com/world/2017/nov/21/after-the-liberation-of-mosul-an-orgy-of-killing

Arendt, Hannah (2006 [1965]) *On Revolution*, ed. Jonathan Schell. New York: Penguin.

Atack, Iain (2012) *Nonviolence in Political Theory*. Edinburgh: Edinburgh University Press.

BBC (2014) 'Ethics Guide: Ethics of War', archived webpage: http://www.bbc.co.uk/ethics/war/

Benbaji, Yitzhak (2008) 'A Defense of the Traditional War Convention', *Ethics* 118: 464–95.

Benbaji, Yitzhak (2009) 'The War Convention and the Moral Division of Labour', *Philosophical Quarterly* 59: 593–617.

Benbaji, Yitzhak (2011) 'The Moral Power of Soldiers to Undertake the Duty of Obedience', *Ethics* 122: 43–73.

References

Bellamy, Alex (2006) *Just Wars: From Cicero to Iraq*. Cambridge: Polity.

Biggar, Nigel (2013a) *In Defence of War*. Oxford: Oxford University Press.

Biggar, Nigel (2013b) 'Christian Just War Reasoning and Two Cases of Rebellion: Ireland 1916–1921 and Syria 2011–Present', *Ethics and International Affairs* 27(4): 393–400.

Brunstetter, Daniel R. and O'Driscoll, Cian (2017) *Just War Thinkers: from Cicero to the Twenty-First Century*. Abingdon: Routledge.

Buchanan, Allen (2006) 'Institutionalizing the Just War', *Philosophy and Public Affairs,* 34(1): 2–38.

Buchanan, Allen (2013) 'The Ethics of Revolution and its Implications for the Ethics of Intervention', *Philosophy and Public Affairs* 41(3): 292–323.

Buchanan, Allen (2018) 'A Richer *Jus ad Bellum*', in Seth Lazar and Helen Frowe (eds), *The Oxford Handbook of the Ethics of War*. Oxford: Oxford University Press.

Burleigh, Michael (2010) *Moral Combat: A History of World War II*. London: Harper Press.

Burns, Ken and Novick, Lynn (2017) *The Vietnam War*, television documentary series, first shown September–October 2017, BBC Four.

Byman, Daniel (2015) 'Beyond Counterterrorism: Washington Needs a Real Middle East Policy', *Foreign Affairs* 94(6): 11–18.

Cameron, David (2015) 'Memorandum to the Foreign Affairs Select Committee', https://www.parliament.

uk/documents/commons-committees/foreign-affairs/
PM-Response-to-FAC-Report-Extension-of-Offensive-
British-Military-Operations-to-Syria.pdf

Caney, Simon (2005) *Justice Beyond Borders: A Global Political Theory*. Oxford: Oxford University Press.

Childress, James F. (1978) 'Just-War Theories: The Bases, Interrelations, Priorities, and Functions of their Criteria', *Theological Studies* 39(3): 427–45.

Coady, C. A. J. (2008) *Morality and Political Violence*. New York: Cambridge University Press.

Coates, A. J. (2008) 'Is the Independent Application of *Jus in Bello* the Way to Limit War?', in David Rodin and Henry Shue (eds), *Just and Unjust Warriors: The Moral and Legal Status of Soldiers*. Oxford: Oxford University Press.

Cordall, Simon Speakman (2014) 'How Syria's Assad Helped Forge ISIS', *Newsweek*, 21 June, http://www.newsweek.com/how-syrias-assad-helped-forge-isis-255631

DellaPergola, Sergio (1993) 'Jews in the European Community: Sociodemographic Trends and Challenges', *American Jewish Year Book* 93: 25–82.

Department of Justice (USA) (2011) 'White Paper on Targeted Killing', http://msnbcmedia.msn.com/i/msnbc / sections / news / 020413 _ DOJ _ White _ Paper.pdf

Dower, Nigel (2009) *The Ethics of War and Peace: Cosmopolitan and Other Perspectives*. Cambridge: Polity.

References

Draper, Kai (2015) *War and Individual Rights: The Foundations of Just War Theory*. New York: Oxford University Press.

Elshtain, Jean Bethke (1982) 'On Beautiful Souls, Just Warriors, and Feminist Consciousness', *Women's Studies International Forum* 5 (3/4): 341–8.

Fabre, Cécile (2008) 'Cosmopolitanism, Just War Theory, and Legitimate Authority', *International Affairs* 84(5): 963–76.

Fabre, Cécile (2012) *Cosmopolitan War*. Oxford: Oxford University Press.

Fabre, Cécile (2016) *Cosmopolitan Peace*. Oxford: Oxford University Press.

Fabre, Cécile and Lazar, Seth (eds) (2015) *The Morality of Defensive War*. Oxford: Oxford University Press.

Ferguson, Niall (2006) *The War of the World: History's Age of Hatred*. London: Penguin.

Fiala, Andrew (2008) *The Just War Myth*. Lanham: Rowman and Littlefield.

Fiala, Andrew (2014) 'Pacifism', in Edward N. Zalta (ed.), *The Stanford Encyclopedia of Philosophy* (Winter edn), https://plato.stanford.edu/archives/win2014/entries/pacifism/

Finlay, Christopher J. (2010) 'Legitimacy and Non-State Political Violence', *Journal of Political Philosophy* 18(3): 287–312.

Finlay, Christopher J. (2015) *Terrorism and the Right to Resist: A Theory of Just Revolutionary War*. Cambridge: Cambridge University Press.

References

Finlay, Christopher J. (2017a) 'Bastards, Brothers, and Unjust Warriors: Ethics and Enmity in Just War Cinema', *Review of International Studies* 43(1): 73–94.

Finlay, Christopher J. (2017b) 'The Perspective of the Rebel: A Gap in the Global Normative Architecture', *Ethics and International Affairs* 31(2): 213–34.

Finlay, Christopher J. (2018) 'The Deadly Serious Causes of Legitimate Rebellion: Between the Wrongs of Terrorism and the Crimes of War', *Criminal Law and Philosophy* 12(2): 271–87.

FitzPatrick, William (2012) 'The Doctrine of Double Effect: Intention and Permissibility', *Philosophy Compass* 7(3): 183–96.

Frowe, Helen (2014) *Defensive Killing.* Oxford: Oxford University Press.

Gat, Azar (2017) *The Causes of War and the Spread of Peace: But will War Rebound?* Oxford: Oxford University Press.

Gniazdowski, Mateusz (2007) 'Losses Inflicted on Poland by Germany during World War II. Assessments and Estimates – an Outline', *Polish Quarterly of International Affairs* 1: 94–126.

Gray, John (2014) 'ISIS: An Apocalyptic Cult Carving a Place in the Modern World', *The Guardian*, 24 August, https://www.theguardian.com/commentisfree/2014/aug/26/isis-apocalyptic-cult-carving-place-in-modern-world

References

Grotius, Hugo (2012 [1625]) *On the Law of War and Peace*, ed. Stephen C. Neff. Cambridge: Cambridge University Press.

Grynaviski, Eric (2016) 'Intending War Rightly: Right Intentions, Public Intentions, and Consent', *Review of International Studies* 42(4): 634–53.

Hansard (2015) House of Commons, Parliamentary Debates, 2 December, https://publications.parliament.uk/pa/cm201516/cmhansrd/cm151202/debtext/151202-0002.htm

Haque, Adil Ahmad (2017) *Law and Morality at War*. Oxford: Oxford University Press.

Hathaway, Oona and Shapiro, Scott (2017) *The Internationalists and their Plan to Outlaw War*. London: Penguin.

Hobbes, Thomas (1996 [1651]), *Leviathan*, ed. Richard Tuck. Cambridge: Cambridge University Press.

Holmes, Robert (2017) *Pacifism: A Philosophy of Nonviolence*. London: Bloomsbury.

Howes, Dustin Ells (2015) 'The Just War Masquerade', *Peace Review* 27(3): 379–87.

Hutchings, Kimberly (2018) 'War and Moral Stupidity', *Review of International Studies* 44(1): 83–100.

Iser, Mattias (2017) 'Beyond the Paradigm of Self-Defense? On Revolutionary Violence', in Saba Bazargan-Forward and Samuel C. Rickless (eds), *The Ethics of War: Essays*. New York: Oxford University Press.

Johnson, James Turner (1975) *Ideology, Reason, and the*

Limitation of War: Religious and Secular Concepts, 1200–1740. Princeton: Princeton University Press.

Johnson, James Turner (1981) *Just War Tradition and the Restraint of War: A Moral and Historical Inquiry*. Princeton: Princeton University Press.

Johnson, James Turner (1999) *Morality and Contemporary Warfare*. New Haven: Yale University Press.

Johnson, James Turner (2013) 'Contemporary Just War Thinking: Which is Worse, to Have Friends or Critics?', *Ethics and International Affairs* 27(1): 25–45.

Joint Committee of the UK House of Commons and House of Lords on Human Rights (2016) 'The Government's Policy on the Use of Drones for Targeted Killing' (Second Report of Session 2015–16).

Judt, Tony (2010) *Postwar: A History of Europe since 1945*. London: Vintage.

Kalmanowitz, Pablo (2018) 'Sovereignty, Pluralism, and Regular War: Wolff and Vattel's Enlightenment Critique of Just War', *Political Theory* 46(2): 218–41.

Kershaw, Ian (2015) *To Hell and Back: Europe, 1914–1949*. London: Penguin.

Kettle, Martin (2015) 'Hilary Benn's Speech on Syria Could Transform Labour', *The Guardian*, 3 December, https://www.theguardian.com/commentisfree/2015/dec/03/hilary-benn-speech-syria-labour-mps-war

Kochi, Tarik (2009) *The Other's War: Recognition and the Violence of Ethics*. London: Birkbeck Law Press.

References

Kochi, Tarik (2013) 'Problems of Legitimacy within the Just War Tradition and International Law', in Anthony F. Lang, Cian O'Driscoll and John Williams (eds), *Just War: Authority, Tradition, and Practice*. Washington DC: Georgetown University Press.

Kuhn, Thomas (1996 [1962]) *The Structure of Scientific Revolutions*, 3rd edn. Chicago: Chicago University Press.

Lang, Anthony F., Jr (2016) 'Just War as Political Theory: Intention, Cause and Authority', *Political Theory* 44(2): 289–303.

Lazar, Seth (2012) 'Necessity in Self-Defence and War', *Philosophy and Public Affairs* 40(1): 3–44.

Lazar, Seth (2015) *Sparing Civilians*. Oxford: Oxford University Press.

Lazar, Seth (2017a) 'Just War Theory: Revisionists versus Traditionalists', *Annual Review of Political Science* 20: 37–54.

Lazar, Seth (2017b) 'War', in Edward N. Zalta (ed.), *The Stanford Encyclopedia of Philosophy* (Spring edn), https://plato.stanford.edu/archives/spr2017/entries/war/

Leitenberg, Milton (2006) 'Deaths in Wars and Conflicts in the 20th Century', Cornell University Peace Studies Programme Occasional Paper 29 (3rd edn), https://www.clingendael.org/sites/default/files/pdfs/20060800_cdsp_occ_leitenberg.pdf

Linklater, Andrew (2017) *Violence and Civilization in*

the Western States System. Cambridge: Cambridge University Press.

Locke, John (1988 [1689]) *Two Treatise of Government*, ed. Peter Laslett. Cambridge: Cambridge University Press.

Luban, David (2004) 'Preventive War', *Philosophy and Public Affairs* 32(3): 207–48.

Luban, David (2011) 'War as Punishment', *Philosophy and Public Affairs* 39(4): 299–330.

Machiavelli, Niccolò (1998) *The Prince*, 2nd edn, trans. Harvey C. Mansfield. Chicago: University of Chicago Press.

Machiavelli, Niccolò (2003 [1521]) *The Art of War*, trans. Christopher Lynch. Chicago: Chicago University Press.

Malcolm, Noel (2002) *Aspects of Hobbes*. Oxford: Clarendon Press.

Manna, Haytham (2012) 'Syria's Opposition has been Led Astray by Violence', *The Guardian*, 22 June, https://www.theguardian.com/commentisfree/2012/jun/22/syria-opposition-led-astray-by-violence

May, Larry (2008) *Aggression and Crimes Against Peace*. New York: Cambridge University Press.

May, Larry (2015) *Contingent Pacifism*. Cambridge: Cambridge University Press.

McIntyre, Alison (2014) 'Doctrine of Double Effect', in Edward N. Zalta (ed.), *The Stanford Encyclopedia of Philosophy* (Winter edn), https://plato.stanford.edu/archives/win2014/entries/double-effect/

References

McMahan, Jeff (2003) *The Ethics of Killing: Problems at the Margins of Life*. New York: Oxford University Press.

McMahan, Jeff (2005) 'Just Cause for War', *Ethics and International Affairs* 19(3): 1–21.

McMahan, Jeff (2007) '*Just War*', in Robert E. Goodin, Philip Pettit and Thomas Pogge (eds), *A Companion to Contemporary Political Philosophy*, 2nd edn, Oxford: Blackwell.

McMahan, Jeff (2009) *Killing in War*. Oxford: Clarendon Press.

Mill, John Stuart (1984 [1859]) 'A Few Words on Non-Intervention', in John M. Robson (ed.), *The Collected Works of John Stuart Mill*, vol. XXI. Toronto: Toronto University Press.

National Conference of Catholic Bishops, USA (1983) 'The Challenge of Peace: God's Promise and Our Response; A Pastoral Letter on War and Peace', http://www.usccb.org/issues-and-action/human-life-and-dignity/war-and-peace/nuclear-weapons/upload/statement-the-challenge-of-peace-1983-05-03.pdf

Neff, Stephen C. (2005) *War and the Law of Nations: A General History*. Cambridge: Cambridge University Press.

Nickel, James (2017) 'Human Rights', in Edward N. Zalta (ed.), *The Stanford Encyclopedia of Philosophy* (Spring edn), https://plato.stanford.edu/archives/spr2017/entries/rights-human/

References

Norman, Richard (1995) *Ethics, Killing, and War*. Cambridge: Cambridge University Press.

Obama, Barack (2009) Nobel Peace Prize Speech, http://swampland.time.com/2009/12/10/barack-obamas-nobel-prize-speech-transcript/

OHCHR (Office of the UN High Commissioner for Human Rights) (2016) 'Out of Sight, Out of Mind: Deaths in Detention in the Syrian Arab Republic', 3 February, http://www.ohchr.org/Documents/HRBodies/HRCouncil/CoISyria/A-HRC-31-CRP1_en.pdf

Orend, Brian (2013) *The Morality of War*, 2nd edn. Peterborough, Ontario: Broadview Press.

Overy, Richard (2013) *The Bombing War: Europe 1939–45*. London: Penguin.

Parry, Jonathan (2017) 'Legitimate Authority and the Ethics of War: A Map of the Terrain', *Ethics and International Affairs* 31(2): 169–89.

Parry, Jonathan (2018) 'Civil War and Revolution', in Helen Frowe and Seth Lazar (eds), *The Oxford Handbook of Ethics and War*. Oxford: Oxford University Press.

Pattison, James (2015) 'The Ethics of British Intervention in Syria', *Manchester Policy Blogs*, 4 December, http://blog.policy.manchester.ac.uk/posts/2015/12/the-ethics-of-british-intervention-in-syria/

Pattison, James (2018) 'The Case for the Nonideal Morality of War: Beyond Revisionism versus Traditionalism in Just War Theory', *Political Theory* 46(2): 242–68.

Pinker, Steven (2012) *The Better Angels of Our Nature: A History of Violence and Humanity*. London: Penguin.

Rawls, John (1971) *A Theory of Justice*. Cambridge MA: Harvard University Press.

Rawls, John (1999) *The Law of Peoples*. Cambridge, MA: Harvard University Press.

Reichberg, Gregory (2008) 'Jus ad Bellum', in Larry May with Mary Crookston (eds), *War: Essays in Political Philosophy*. New York: Cambridge University Press.

Reichberg, Gregory, Syse, Henrik and Begby, Endre (eds) (2006) *The Ethics of War: Classic and Contemporary Readings*. Oxford: Blackwell.

Reitberger, Magnus (2013) 'License to Kill: Is Legitimate Authority a Requirement for Just War?', *International Theory* 5(1): 64–93.

Rengger, Nicholas (2013) *Just War and International Order: The Uncivil Condition in World Politics*. Cambridge: Cambridge University Press.

Rodin, David (2002) *War and Self-Defense*. Oxford: Oxford University Press.

Rodin, David and Shue, Henry (eds) (2008) *Just and Unjust Warriors: The Moral and Legal Status of Soldiers*. Oxford: Oxford University Press.

Ryan, Cheyney (2018) 'Pacifism', in Helen Frowe and Seth Lazar (eds), *The Oxford Handbook of Ethics and War*. Oxford: Oxford University Press.

Schmitt, Carl (2011 [1937]) 'The Turn to the Discriminating Concept of War', in Timothy Nunan (ed.), *Writings on War*. Cambridge: Polity.

References

Sherman, Nancy (2005) *Stoic Warriors: The Ancient Philosophy Behind the Military Mind*. New York: Oxford University Press.

Sjoberg, Laura (2006) *Gender, Justice, and the Wars in Iraq: A Feminist Reformulation of Just War Theory*. Lanham: Lexington Books.

Slim, Randa (2011) 'Meet Syria's Opposition', *Foreign Policy*, 2 November, http://foreignpolicy.com/2011/11/02/meet-syrias-opposition/

Slomp, Gabriella (2005) 'The Theory of the Partisan: Carl Schmitt's Neglected Legacy', *History of Political Thought* 26(3): 502–19.

Slomp, Gabriella (2006) 'Carl Schmitt's Five Arguments Against the Idea of Just War', *Cambridge Review of International Affairs* 19(3): 435–47.

Statman, Daniel (2008) 'On the Success Condition for Legitimate Self-Defence', *Ethics* 118: 659–86.

Steinhoff, Uwe (2007) *The Ethics of War and Terrorism*. Oxford: Oxford University Press.

Syrian Network for Human Rights (2015) 'The Main Conflict Parties who are Killing Civilians in Syria', http://sn4hr.org/wp-content/pdf/english/Who_Are_Killing_Civilians_in_Syria_en.pdf

Teschke, Benno (2016) 'Carl Schmitt's Concepts of War: A Categorical Failure', in Jens Meierhenrich and Oliver Simons (eds), *The Oxford Handbook of Carl Schmitt*. Oxford: Oxford University Press.

Tolstoy, Leo (1974 [1893]) 'The Kingdom of God is Within You', in *The Kingdom of God and Peace*

Essays, trans. Aylmer Maude. London: Oxford University Press.

Tooze, Adam (2015) *The Deluge: the Great War and the Remaking of the Global Order, 1916–31*. London: Penguin.

Tooze, Adam (2016) '1917 – 365 Days that Shook the World', *Prospect*, 13 December.

Vitoria, Francisco (1991 [1539]) 'On the Law of War', in A. R. Pagden and Jeremy Lawrence (eds), *Vitoria: Political Writings*. Cambridge: Cambridge University Press.

Waldron, Jeremy (2010) 'Civilians, Terrorism, and Deadly Serious Conventions', in *Torture, Terror and Trade-Offs: Philosophy for the Whitehouse*. Oxford: Oxford University Press.

Waltz, Kenneth (1959) *Man, the State, and War*. New York: Columbia University Press.

Walzer, Michael (1971) 'World War II: Why Was This War Different?', *Philosophy and Public Affairs* 1(1): 3–21.

Walzer, Michael (1977) *Just and Unjust Wars: A Moral Argument with Historical Illustrations*. New York: Basic Books.

Walzer, Michael (2004) *Arguing About War*. New Haven, CT: Yale University Press.

Walzer, Michael (2013) 'Were We Wrong about Syria?', *Dissent*, blog, 30 October, https://www.dissentmagazine.org/blog/were-we-wrong-about-syria

Walzer, Michael (2015) 'What Kind of a War Is This?' *Dissent*, blog, 3 December, https://www.dissentmaga

zine.org/blog/france-us-uk-air-strikes-ISIS-just-war-theory

Weber, Max (2004 [1919]) 'Politics as a Vocation', in David Owen and Tracy B. Strong (eds), *The Vocation Lectures*. Indianapolis: Hackett Publishing.

Williams, John (2006) *The Ethics of Territorial Borders: Drawing Lines in the Shifting Sand*. Basingstoke: Palgrave Macmillan.

Wintour, Patrick, Chulov, Martin and Black, Ian (2016) 'Russian Bombs Triggering Mass Aleppo Exodus, Syria Conference Told', *The Guardian*, 4 February, https://www.theguardian.com/world/2016/feb/04/russian-bombs-trigger-mass-aleppo-exodus-syria-conference-told

Witt, John Fabian (2012) *Lincoln's Code: The Laws of War in American History*. New York: Free Press.

Wood, Graeme (2015) 'What ISIS Really Wants', *The Atlantic*, March, https://www.theatlantic.com/magazine/archive/2015/03/what-isis-really-wants/384980/

Zurbuchen, Simone (2009) 'Vattel's Law of Nations and Just War Theory', *History of European Ideas* 35(4): 408–7.